The Original
Salt-Free
Diet Cookbook

The Original Salt-Free Diet Cookbook

Emil G. Conason, M.D.
and
Ella Metz, Dietitian

A Perigee Book

Acknowledgments

The authors would like to express their thanks to Rose Anne Salvino for her diligent research and help in creating the recipes for this revised edition.

Perigee Books
are published by
The Putnam Publishing Group
200 Madison Avenue
New York, NY 10016

Library of Congress Cataloging-in-Publication Data

Conason, Emil G.
  The original salt-free diet cookbook.

  Reprint. Originally published: The salt-free diet
cook book. New York: Lear, 1949.
    1. Salt-free diet—Recipes. 2. Reducing diets—
Recipes. I. Metz, Ella. II. Title.
RM237.8.C66   1986   641.5′632   85-25959
ISBN 0-399-51231-4

Printed in the United States of America
1 2 3 4 5 6 7 8 9 10

Contents

INTRODUCTION TO THE
FIRST EDITION

The body fluids of man contain precisely 0.85 percent of salt. This percentage of salt is maintained in the blood of all healthy individuals. Any radical change in its proportion will cause catastrophic, life-threatening changes in the blood elements. A marked increase in concentration in the blood causes the red blood cells to shrink and wrinkle. A lowering of the normal percentage causes swelling and then rupture of the red blood cells.

Common table salt, chemically, is sodium chloride. A molecule of salt is made up of an atom of sodium joined to an atom of chlorine. This chemical combination formed by the union of the soft, lustrous, silver-like metal, sodium, and the greenish yellow, acrid, poisonous gas, chlorine, has always been considered one of the most innocuous of all the substances consumed by living matter. Practically all living matter contains salt. Without it life would seem to be impossible. In many parts of the world there are great salt licks to which the local wildlife periodically is attracted to replenish its salt needs. Some powerful instinct seems to lead animals to the salt supply. Among some of the pygmy tribes of Africa whose normal terrain is lacking in salt, the mineral has become a prized symbol of wealth and a means of exchange.

The exchange of foods and waste materials by the living cells of the body depends upon the concentration of sodium on the cell membrane. Any shift of serious proportions in the body's salt concentration causes interference with normal metabolism of the cells and eventually causes death of the tissues themselves. Research has shown that it is the sodium ion and not the chloride ion which is responsible for water retention in the body. The mechanism by which the concentration of salt is kept at the physiological point is by way of the kidneys. If salt tends to increase in concentration in the blood, urination increases and the excess salt is excreted through the urine. Any tendency to dropping of the salt level of the blood is offset by kidney retention. The ability of the kidney to keep the salt concentration in balance depends in its turn on the functioning of the adrenal cortex gland. This gland excretes hormones into the blood which tend (among other things) to keep the ratio of sodium, potassium and calcium at the proper level. In disease involving the adrenal cortex, the heart, the liver, or the kidney itself, the normal balance of the body sodium is violently changed. With the change in sodium balance, a resulting change in water balance also occurs. The tissue spaces become water-logged or edematous. Fluids gather in unaccustomed places; organs are swollen out of all proportion; their functions interfered with; and a vicious cycle of degeneration is set up. The swollen kidney or liver or brain fails to function properly. The edematous adrenal cortex is less able to bring about the normal kidney exchange; the heart finds difficulty in pumping the blood through the water-logged tissue spaces; cellular respiration is interfered with; tissues die. Whichever organ system is initially at fault, all organs and all body tissues are finally involved unless some way is found to restore the balance and clear the body of the retained sodium and its attendant water.

The healthy individual, averaging 150 pounds, normally excretes 10 to 15 grams (10,000–15,000 milligrams) of sodium chloride every 24 hours (since sodium constitutes roughly 51 percent of sodium chloride, that is, 5 to 8 grams of sodium per day). It is obvious that to do this he must consume in his food and drink a similar quantity of sodium chloride. As I have remarked above, in the healthy individual any sudden increase in the daily sodium intake results in an increased output of salt by way of the urine; likewise, a marked diminution in the intake of sodium results in retention by the kidneys and a decrease in urination. Not so in those whose physiological mechanisms are unbalanced. In the sick, salt often tends to accumulate and to hold water in the tissue spaces. From the point of advantage of the backward glance one is tempted to express amazement at the failure of medical science to recognize earlier the importance of regulating sodium intake in the control of such conditions as:

1. Dropsy (the edema of cardiac failure)
2. Nephritis
3. Nephrosis
4. The edema of liver cirrhosis
5. Meniere's syndrome (ringing in the ears and dizziness)
6. Eclampsia (the toxemia of pregnancy)
7. In premenstrual syndrome
8. Migraine
9. Epilepsy
10. In intractable insomnia and nervous tension states
11. Rheumatic arthritic swelling
12. Hypertension (high blood pressure)
13. Reducing diets

However, it was not until the early 1920s that attention was called to the possibility of breaking the vicious cycle of sodium and water retention and imbalance. In the same year (1922) that saw the mass commercial production of insulin for diabetics, Dr. Frederick M. Allen and his coworkers announced the use of a diet low in sodium chloride as a treatment for hypertension (high blood pressure). This group treated 280 patients suffering with very severe, otherwise uncontrollable, high blood pressure with a diet in which the sodium content was held down to 150 milligrams. They followed their cases for a period of over four years. They were convinced that those who adhered to the diet were vastly improved in health and that their lives had been greatly prolonged.

Allen's follow-up of the low-sodium diet treatment of severe hypertensives in the past quarter century had so completely convinced him of the value of the treatment that he summed up his experiences in a discussion reported in the *Journal of the American Medical Association,* June 4, 1949, page 462. Recognizing the fact that there were a few patients who were refractory to treatment, Allen went on to say: "Just as in diabetes, failure in worst cases do not invalidate diet principle. My distinction twenty-two years ago between symptom and disease of hypertension, explains benefits, not merely measured by pressure reduction and often apparent after years in initially refractory cases. . . . Diet keeps all but extremely hypertensive patients active and improved. Frequent clearing of retinitis (swelling of the retina and optic nerve of the eye), congestive failure (heart failure), headache, dyspnea (shortness of breath) and other symptoms is unmistakable. . . . Appetizing diet encourages fidelity. Long ago, the public should have been taught to accept diet for hypertension as routinely as for diabetes. The waste of life during the past twenty years may continue for another ten years before all agree. My conclusion, based on unique experience in several thousand cases during twenty-eight years, is that saltless diet, especially when begun reasonably early, can specifically *arrest progressiveness, prevent complications,* and thus provide the first real control of deaths from hypertension."

During the past few years there has been a new flurry of attention to the use of the low-sodium diet in high blood pressure. Dr. Walter Kempner, assistant professor of clinical medicine at Duke University, Durham, N.C., has enthusiastically reported great success in the treatment of patients with high blood pressure by the so-called Rice Diet. In this diet, as in Dr. Allen's diet, the sodium content is held down to 150 milligrams. At a meeting of the New York Heart Association, Nov. 16, 1948, Dr. Kempner reported the results in his treatment of 700 patients. His Rice Diet was given to these patients for periods ranging between 35 and 900 days. He has reported beneficial effects in 70 percent of his patients.

THE RICE DIET

Dr. Kempner's diet is called the Rice Diet because it is based upon rice as one of its main constituents. The diet contains in some 2000 calories only 20 grams of protein and 5 grams of fat per day. As mentioned above no more than 150 milligrams of sodium is permitted in the 24 hours. The rice, which forms the backbone of the diet, may be brown, polished or wild. Fruit is used to supplement the rice. So long as it is unsalted, the fruit may be raw, stewed, canned, dried, frozen or preserved. Nuts, dates and avocados are forbidden. While brown or white sugar or honey may be used none of the ordinary commercial syrups, such as Karo or maple syrup are permitted. Vegetable juices are *NOT* included. Fluids are limited to a pint and a half to two pints of fruit juices (canned or fresh). The following supplement completes the diet:

Vitamin A	5000	units
Vitamin D	1000	units
Riboflavin	5	milligrams
Thiamin Chloride	5	milligrams
Niacinamide	25	milligrams
Ferrous Sulphate	0.6	milligram

Dr. Kempner has stated that while the usual caloric intake of the patients is restricted to 2000 calories, it is often necessary to vary the calories according to the patient's need to gain or lose weight. He points out that the average time required for attaining a marked decrease in blood pressure is between three and four months. He has seen marked decreases in as little as four days. An occasional patient has taken 12 months. Dr. Kempner has claimed that the Rice Diet, under his supervision, has resulted in significant *reduction in the size of greatly enlarged hearts* and that *the edema* (water logging of the tissues) *due to kidney disease was eliminated.* He has also commented on favorable changes in electrocardiograms and favorable changes in the fundus of the eye (retina and optic nerve head). In Dr. Kempner's papers the striking effects of the Rice Diet on heart size, blood pressure, electrocardiographic markings and on the ocular fundi have been seen most often in patients with congestive heart failure or nephritis.

Other Low-Sodium Diets

The diets of both Allen and Kempner are so rigid that they are not feasible in the ambulatory patient. Dr. Milton Landowne and his coworkers (*Journal of the American Medical Association,* June 4, 1949, page 462) undertook to study a group of patients who were ambulatory. They put these patients on a diet limited to 300 milligrams of sodium per day. Unknown to the patient he was given 2 grams (2000 milligrams) of sodium a day in a capsule. Urinary studies of sodium output showed that only *one in three patients* stayed within the limits of the diet despite the fact that their actual daily sodium intake was far beyond that permitted in the Rice Diet or in Allen's diet. Their sodium intake was more than 2300 milligrams per day. It would seem obvious that such results as Allen and Kempner achieved can be reproduced only under the rigid supervision made possible by hospital care.

Nevertheless a number of reports have been made on the advantages and beneficial effects of other low-sodium diets in various conditions. For instance, M. H. Barker has reported on the beneficial effects in patients with congestive heart failure of a diet containing 1000 milligrams of sodium a day (*Journal of the American Medical Association,* June 1932). F. R. Schemm in the *Annals of Internal Medicine,* Dec. 1942, has reported benefit in cardiac edema patients with a diet containing somewhat over 1000 milligrams of sodium per day.

The famous Karrell Diet, which consisted of 4 glasses of milk with 8 slices of dry salt-free toasted bread per day, was used in cardiac and nephritic edema with great success by the doctors of the early twentieth century. Its benefits might well have been due to the fact that the total sodium intake of such a diet is about 600 milligrams.

Wheeler, Bridges and White (*Journal of the American Medical Association,* Jan 4, 1947, pages 16–20) treated congestive heart failure in a series of 50 patients with a diet containing about 625 milligrams of sodium. Their patients were selected because of their refractoriness to previous therapy. Of the 50 patients, 35 had faithfully followed the diet. Of these 22 were improved, 13 showed no improvement. Walsh and Adson (*Journal of the American Medical Association,* Jan 13, 1940, pages 130–136) treated 128 patients suffering with Meniere's syndrome on low-sodium diet. They gave their patients ammonium chloride to increase urinary output. Forty-five of these patients were completely relieved of their vertigo. Thirty-three reported vertigo improved. Fifty patients found no improvement. M. M. Miller (*Journal of the American Medical Association,* Sept. 22, 1945, pages 262–266) treated 20 patients suffering from insomnia and nervous tension. He used a diet restricted to 2 grams (2000 milligrams) of sodium chloride a day. Seventeen of these patients reported that their symptoms disappeared under treatment. When 13 of these patients were placed on a normal salt intake, relapses occurred in 10 of them.

K. De Snoo, in the *American Journal of Obstetrics and Gynecology,* Dec. 1937, implicated sodium as the cause of the eclampsia of pregnancy. He advocated a low-salt diet in pregnant women during the second half of pregnancy. J. O. Arnold, in the *Medical Clinics of North America,* July 1934, had suggested the limitation of salt in the diet of pregnant women threatened with eclampsia.

W. Pomerance and I. Daichman, *American Journal of Obstetrics and Gynecology,* Dec. 1940, have made the interesting observation that the length of labor is apparently reduced by a low-salt diet in the latter part of pregnancy. Greenhill and Fried, *Journal of the American Medical Association,* Aug. 16, 1941, and Thorn et al., *Endocrinology,* Feb. 1938, found benefit in low-sodium diets in the edema and tension of the so-called premenstrual state.

How These Menus Should Be Used

It is of course assumed that patients who are in need of the low-sodium menus outlined in this book are under the care of a competent doctor. The patient is strongly urged to check frequently with his doctor. The constant check-up is just as important in the low-sodium diet as it is in diabetes. In such conditions as Addison's disease, a disease of the adrenal cortex, sodium deprivation may actually initiate collapse. Occasional urine analysis for sodium or chloride content will guide the doctor in his prescription of the various sodium levels. For instance, in the case of the cardiac patient whose water retention has been relieved by rigid adherence to the Rice Diet, the doctor may find it desirable to raise the sodium content to a 300 milligram level per day for maintenance; likewise in patients with nephrosis, Meniere's syndrome, and even hypertension. Surely the eclamptic patient who has been delivered of her child will want her sodium intake allowance raised to the highest point consistent with good health. The division of our suggested menus at varying sodium levels is meant to be of assistance to the doctor in his prescribing. We suggest that the doctor use his judgment in varying the menus, eliminating where he finds it desirable, combining elements from each group and improvising where he finds it possible to take the time. To take but a simple example, the elimination in our Menu I for breakfast of ½ cup of milk reduces the sodium content of the breakfast from 81.4 to 23.4 milligrams of sodium.

We have attempted to make this book a manual of convenience for both the doctor and the patient. Our special menus for the diabetic who requires low-sodium intake, for the person who eats out, for the obese patient who requires weight reduction are each subject to interchange and modification. For the doctor who wishes to make his own changes we have added a table at the end of the book of the sodium content of hundreds of the commonly used basic foods. It will be noted that four authorities, whose findings are extremely divergent as to sodium content of the same foods, are quoted. This has not been done with the intent to confuse the reader. The confusion among scientists and in the scientific literature, and the difference in chemical estimation, have been due to the fact that until recently there were no accurate tests available for the estimation of sodium as such. The various scientific writers on diet and nutrition were forced to make highly inaccurate indirect estimates of sodium content. This was usually done by careful chemical estimations of the chlorides present. From the chloride content the sodium content was then assumed. We have found the book, *The Chemical Composition of Foods* by R. A. McCance and E. M. Widdowson published by the Chemical Publishing Co., Inc., Brooklyn, N. Y., fairly consistent and in general agreement with the figures quoted in the special brochure published by Mead Johnson & Co., Evansville 21, Indiana entitled *Sodium and Potassium Analysis of Foods and Waters.* The figures quoted by Mead Johnson were obtained by the special process of flame photometry. The analysis was made by their own research laboratories. Wherever we have used a figure in which there was disagreement between these two authorities, we have taken the higher figure on the assumption that it was desirable to err if necessary on the side of a lower rather than a higher sodium content. Where either of these two authorities failed to give the figure for sodium in a food, we have resorted to *Chemistry of Food and Nutrition,* by Henry C.Sherman, Ph.D., Sc.D., published by the Macmillan Co., New York, and on *Elements of Food Biochemistry* by Peterson, Skinner and Strong, published by Prentice-Hall, Inc., New York.

Throughout the book we have placed side by side the caloric value and the sodium value in milligrams per ounce of the various foods and combinations we have used. We have expressed these measurements in milligrams per ounce and in calories per ounce. For the benefit of those who prefer to use the metric system throughout rather than the hybrid method we have chosen, milligrams per ounce as well as calories per ounce may be roughly translated to milligrams and calories per hundred grams by merely multiplying each of our figures by 30.

Most recipes are given in single portion quantities unless otherwise stated. Wherever, in the menus, recipes are given for certain dishes, the fact is denoted by the presence of an asterisk after the name of the dish.

The preparation of palatable menus for the patient requiring sodium restriction was far from simple. In attempting to treat a number of patients who found it impossible to adhere to the stringent rigidities of the Rice Diet, I discovered the lack of any available source of information for the patient's use. As patient after patient complained of the colorlessness and inanity of the diets I prescribed, and as their urine chloride tests showed more and more frequent lapses in their adherence to the diet, the need for this book became apparent.

My colleague, Miss Ella Metz, undertook to work out a practical, kitchen-wise, helpful series of more interesting menus to meet this need. Each of the dishes has been actually prepared and served to a member of her family in need of low-sodium diet. This book is the result.

EMIL G. CONASON, M.D.

Table of Measurements

All measurements are given as level measurements.

3 teaspoons	1 tablespoon
4 tablespoons	¼ cup
8 tablespoons	½ cup
16 tablespoons	1 cup
1 cup	1 glass
2 cups	1 pint
4 cups	1 quart
4 quarts	1 gallon
No. 1 can	1⅓ cup
No. 2 can	2½ cup
No. 2½ can	3½ cup
No. 3 can	4 cup

Table of Weights

1 cup, liquid	8 oz.
2 cups, liquid	1 lb.
2 cups sugar	1 lb.
½ cup butter or 8 T. butter	¼ lb.
4 cups flour	1 lb.
1⅞ cups rice	1 lb.

A Basic Group of Low-Sodium Foods

Beverages

Coca-Cola	Fruit Juices	Tea
Cocoa	Ginger Ale	Wines
Coffee*	Postum	

Condiments

Allspice	Mustard powder	Sage
Caraway	Nutmeg	Thyme
Cinnamon	Paprika	Turmeric
Curry powder	Pepper	Vanilla extract
Garlic	Peppermint extract	Vinegar
Mace		

Avoid onion salt, celery salt and garlic salt. Also avoid all prepared flavorings like prepared horseradish, prepared mustard, Worcestershire sauce, etc.

Fats and Oils

Beef drippings	Crisco	Salad oil
Butter, unsalted	Olive oil	

Avoid margarine, salted butter, bacon fat, and other fats to which salt has been added.

Cereals and Cereal Foods

Arrowroot	Flour—Wheatmeal	Sago
Barley, pearl	Macaroni	Semolina
Cornflour	Maltex	Shredded Wheat
Cracked Wheat	Oatmeal	Soya flour
Cornmeal	Puffed Rice	Tapioca
Farina	Puffed Wheat	Wheatena
Flour—white	Rice	

* Although coffee is a low-sodium food, there is new information and concern about the effect of caffeine in raising the blood pressure. There is some indication that one cup of coffee can raise blood pressure several points. Please check with your doctor.

Dairy Products

Most dairy products are high in sodium. The following are lower than most:

	mg. per oz.		mg. per oz.
Butter	1.4	Egg yolk	14.2
Cream	11.4	Milk	14.5

Meat Products

Most meat products are high-sodium. The following are the ones containing the least amount of sodium.

	mg. per oz.		mg. per oz.
Beef, lean	19.6	Rabbit, foreleg	13.4
Chicken, breast	22.2	Rabbit, loin	9.7
Duck, breast	19.4	Sweetbreads	19.6
Hare	15.0	Tripe	13.1
Lamb, lean	31.4	Turkey, breast	11.4
Liver, beef	24.4	Turkey, leg	26.2
Pig, pancreas	16.2	Veal	30.4
Pigeon	21.0	Venison	24.4
Pork, lean	18.8		

NOTE: Avoid all smoked and processed meats. Frozen meats may be used if not salted.

Fish

All fish except shellfish may be used, with the exception of oysters. Avoid all salted and smoked fish.

Fruits

All fruits and juices, canned or fresh. Avoid those that have sodium benzoate or salt added.

Nuts

All nuts except those that are salted.

Vegetables

Most fresh and canned, except those that have sodium benzoate or salt added. Avoid celery, beets, dandelion, kale, mustard greens, spinach and sauerkraut.

Sugar and Preserves

Chocolate, plain	Honey	Jelly
Cocoanut, dry	Jam	Marmalade
Sugar		

General Rules to Follow in Using Recipes

No salt is to be added to any recipe.

All butter or margarine is to be entirely salt-free.

For shortenings, use only vegetable oils, unsalted butter, unsalted margarine, or unsalted beef drippings.

Canned fruits may be used if no sodium benzoate has been added.

Since canned vegetables are often packed with salt, none are to be used except where noted.

In most cities low-sodium bread may be purchased in chain bakeries. This bread or matzohs may be substituted for the bread recipes on the menus.

Quantities given are for one serving only, unless otherwise stated. Many readers will wish to increase the amounts to save waste, as for example, when ½ egg is required the recipe can be doubled and two portions made.

In boiling, many foods lose some of their sodium. However, this loss is sustained only if the liquor in which the food was boiled is not used.

The drinking of water should be controlled if local water supply is high in sodium. In such instances distilled water may be used.

For greater palatability your doctor may suggest a salt substitute which may be used in the preparation of many of the following menus. Care should be taken to use only as directed by your physician.

MENUS 1–12

400–500 Milligrams of Sodium
1800–2200 Calories

Measurements are expressed in milligrams of sodium and calories in each portion.

MENU 1

Breakfast	Milligrams Sodium	Calories
8 oz. orange juice (1 cup)	4.0	88
¼ cup oatmeal (1 oz.) with	9.5	115
½ cup milk	58.0	76
1 cup coffee† with	—	8
2 t. cream	3.8	38
1 t. sugar	—	19
1 sl. Low-Sodium Bread*	3.5	97
½ T. marmalade or jelly	2.6	37
	81.4	478

Lunch		
Scrambled Eggs and Mushrooms*	81.1	130
Salad—½ banana, ½ sliced apple, 1 large shredded lettuce leaf	5.1	56
Orange Rice Custard*	30.6	409
	116.8	595

(When making Custard, boil 1 T. rice for breakfast tomorrow.)

Dinner		
½ lb. broiled beef liver	195.2	328
1 baked potato, medium	8.0	96
1 t. butter (unsalted)	.2	38
4 oz. String Beans Creole*	15.0	114
Salad—2 oz. lettuce and 1 medium tomato	10.0	22
Vinegar Dressing*	3.0	63
Baked apple with	2.4	40
1 t. sugar and cinnamon	—	19
Coffee†—1 t. sugar and 2 t. cream	3.8	65
	237.6	785
Total for Day	435.8	1858

* Asterisks denote dishes for which recipes are given.
† Decaffeinated coffee may be chosen. It contains 1.7 mg. sodium and 2 calories per cup. With 2 t. milk and 1 t. sugar added, one cup contains 6.5 mg. sodium and 27 calories.

RECIPES FOR MENU 1

Low-Sodium Bread

	Milligrams Sodium	Calories
½ cake yeast (½ oz.)	5	13
½ T. sugar	—	28
½ cup milk	58.5	76
1 T. Crisco (or other vegetable shortening)	—	110
3½ cups flour (about)	9.6	1600
1 T. melted butter	.7	113
½ cup water	—	—
	69.3	1940

Crumble the yeast, and add sugar. Heat the water, milk and shortening together in a saucepan. Add this to the yeast and sugar and mix well. Add half the flour and mix well. Add the remainder of the flour to make a stiff dough. Knead the dough until smooth and place in greased bowl. Spread melted shortening over dough. Cover with towel and let rise in warm place until double in size. Knead again and shape into loaves. Place in well-greased loaf pan and spread with melted shortening. Cover and let rise again until double in bulk. Bake in a moderately hot oven for 1 hour.

This loaf will yield about 20 slices of bread. One slice equals 3.5 mg. sodium and 97 calories.

Scrambled Eggs and Mushrooms

½ cup mushrooms (about 1⅔ oz.)	4.3	3
1 t. butter	.2	38
1 egg	67.0	77
4 t. milk	9.6	12
Pepper	—	—
	81.1	130

Saute mushrooms in butter for a few minutes. Place in top of double boiler. Add egg, milk and pepper. Cook slowly, stirring until creamy.

Orange Rice Custard

	Milligrams Sodium	Calories
1 T. rice	1.2	68
3 T. light cream	17.1	172
2 t. sugar	—	38
4 t. orange juice	.3	8
2 T. heavy cream	11.4	115
¼ orange in sections	.6	8
4 t. water and bit of orange rind	—	—
	30.6	409

Place washed rice, water and light cream in top of double boiler. Cover and steam until rice is tender. Add sugar, orange juice and rind. Cool. Whip heavy cream and fold into the mixture. Pour into cups and chill. Unmold and trim with orange sections.

String Beans Creole

¾ cup string beans (4 oz.)	7.2	16
1 small onion (2 oz.)	5.8	14
½ tomato	1.6	8
2 t. shortening (butter)	.4	76
	15.0	114

Cut one small onion and brown lightly with the shortening. Slice in ½ tomato. Put in string beans and a little water. Cook on small flame until tender (about 20 minutes).

Vinegar Dressing

1 T. vinegar	3.0	—
1 t. olive oil	—	44
1 t. sugar	—	19
	3.0	63

Mix thoroughly.

MENU 2

Breakfast	Milligrams Sodium	Calories
4 oz. orange juice (½ cup) with ½ banana, sliced	2.5	77
1 T. rice (cooked the night before when making Orange Rice Custard)	1.2	68
½ cup milk, hot, with rice	58.0	76
1 t. sugar and cinnamon may be added to milk	—	19
1 sl. Low-Sodium Bread (see Menu 1)	3.5	97
2 t. jelly	4.8	49
Coffee†—2 t. cream and 1 t. sugar	3.8	65
	73.8	451

Lunch		
1 Fried Egg and Mashed Potato*	72.8	249
4 oz. boiled fresh asparagus	2.0	20
1 T. melted butter (unsalted)	.6	114
1 sl. Low-Sodium Toast (see Menu 1)	3.5	97
1 cup fruit salad, canned (4 oz.)	10.0	80
Coffee†—2 t. cream and 1 t. sugar	3.8	65
	92.7	625

Dinner		
½ grapefruit	.8	12
½ lb. broiled shoulder lamb chops, lean only (weighed with fat and bone)	136.0	288
4 oz. fresh peas, boiled	—	56
1 boiled parsley potato	4.0	92
Salad—1 oz. cucumber, ½ tomato, 1 oz. lettuce	8.7	14
4 t. Vinegar Dressing (see Menu 1)	3.0	63
Cocoanut Cream Tapioca*	88.4	326
Coffee†—2 t. cream and 1 t. sugar	3.8	65
	244.7	916
Total for Day	411.2	1992

---

* Asterisks denote dishes for which recipes are given.
† Decaffeinated coffee may be chosen. It contains 1.7 mg. sodium and 2 calories per cup. With 2 t. milk and 1 t. sugar added, one cup contains 6.5 mg. sodium and 27 calories.

RECIPES FOR MENU 2

Fried Eggs and Mashed Potatoes

	Milligrams Sodium	Calories
1 potato, boiled and mashed	4.0	92
1 T. onion, shredded	1.4	4
1 egg	67.0	77
2 t. butter	.4	76
	72.8	249

Fry onions in butter. When onions are browned, remove them and fry eggs in onion-flavored butter. Boil and mash the potato. Garnish the potato with the browned onions and serve with the egg.

Cocoanut Cream Tapioca

(It is best to make this recipe for 4 portions.)

	Milligrams Sodium	Calories
2 t. tapioca (1/3 oz.)	.4	34
1 T. sugar	.5	56
1/4 egg	17.0	19
1 T. shredded cocoanut	1.1	26
1/2 cup milk	58.0	76
2 T. cream	11.4	115
Few drops vanilla	—	—
	88.4	326

Place ingredients, except vanilla and cream, in double boiler and scald. Allow to cook 10 minutes, stirring constantly. Remove from heat. Add vanilla and stir. Allow to cool. Pour into sherbet glass to chill. Top with whipped cream.

MENU 3

Breakfast	Milligrams Sodium	Calories
Mix 4 oz. orange and 4 oz. grapefruit juice	2.4	84
1 Shredded Wheat biscuit (1 oz.) with	4.7	103
½ banana (2½ oz.) with	.7	55
½ cup milk	58.0	76
1 sl. toasted Low-Sodium Bread (see Menu 1) with	3.5	97
1 t. butter (unsalted)	.2	38
Coffee†—2 t. cream and 1 t. sugar	3.8	65
	73.3	518

Lunch		
Spanish Omelet*	93.0	136
1 sl. Low-Sodium Bread	3.5	97
1 t. butter (unsalted)	.2	38
Nut and Apple Tapioca*	8.5	357
Coffee†—1 t. sugar and 2 t. cream	3.8	65
	109.0	693

Dinner		
Salmon Steak*	242.6	487
Baked potato with 1 t. butter	8.2	134
Diced Carrots with Minted Peas*	28.9	65
Hearts of lettuce (2 oz.)	6.8	6
1 T. French Dressing*	—	88
Pineapple and Cocoanut*	3.4	123
	289.9	903
Total for Day	472.2	2114

* Asterisks denote dishes for which recipes are given.
† Decaffeinated coffee may be chosen. It contains 1.7 mg. sodium and 2 calories per cup. With 2 t. milk and 1 t. sugar added, one cup contains 6.5 mg. sodium and 27 calories.

RECIPES FOR MENU 3

Spanish Omelet

	Milligrams Sodium	Calories
1 egg	67.0	77
½ onion (1 oz.)	2.9	7
1 oz. green pepper (3″ piece)	.1	8
½ cup tomatoes (unsalted, 4 oz. canned)	20.4	24
2 fresh mushrooms, peeled and washed (1 oz.)	2.6	2
Few fresh green peas	—	18
	93.0	136

Cut up onion, green pepper. Add tomatoes, green peas and cut-up mushrooms. Cook until soft. Season before serving with a little pepper. Make plain omelet and put in filling when finished.

Nut and Apple Tapioca

2 T. pearl tapioca	.9	68
½ cup water	—	—
1 T. sugar	.5	56
2 T. chopped walnuts	.8	156
1 T. cream	5.7	58
½ t. sugar	—	9
2 T. apples diced (1 oz.)	.6	10
Bit of vanilla	—	—
	8.5	357

Soak tapioca in water for several hours. Add sugar and apples and cook until tapioca is tender and mixture is thick, about 1 hour. Add nuts, cool and serve with sweetened flavored cream.

Salmon Steak

½ lb. fresh salmon (weighed with bones)	197.6	368
2 small mushrooms, chopped fine	2.6	2
½ oz. minced onion	.9	2
1 t. minced parsley		
2 t. butter	.4	76
⅓ wine glass sherry (1 oz.)	2.8	24
1 T. fine bread crumbs (⅕ oz.)	38.3	15
	242.6	487

Sprinkle salmon with mushrooms, onion and parsley. Dot with butter. Add sherry and bake in moderate oven, in shallow baking dish, for 15 minutes. Then sprinkle with the crumbs and continue baking another 15 minutes basting several times.

Diced Carrots with Minted Peas

	Milligrams Sodium	Calories
1 diced carrot (2 oz.)	28.4	10
⅓ cup green peas (2 oz.)	.5	36
½ t. butter	—	19
Bit of mint, crushed	—	—
	28.9	65

Cook diced carrots until tender. Cook peas with crushed mint. When ready to serve combine carrots and peas and melted butter.

French Dressing

Makes ¾ cup.

½ garlic clove	—	—
½ cup olive oil	—	1056
3 T. lemon juice	.6	3
Few grains paprika, few grains pepper	—	—
	.6	1059

One T. equals 88 calories

Make cuts in clove of garlic. Rub bowl with it and then leave it in bowl. Add other ingredients. Stir vigorously with fork. Let stand 30 minutes. Remove garlic. Beat dressing thoroughly. Keep in refrigerator.

Pineapple and Cocoanut

4 oz. canned pineapple chunks	1.1	72
2 T. moist cocoanut (⅐ oz.)	2.3	51
	3.4	123

Mix ingredients thoroughly and serve chilled.

MENU 4

Breakfast	Milligrams Sodium	Calories
8 oz. orange juice	4.0	88
1 cup Puffed Rice (½ oz.)	.1	60
½ cup milk	58.0	76
1 sl. toasted Low-Sodium Bread (see Menu 1)	3.5	97
1 t. butter	.2	38
Coffee†—2 t. cream and 1 t. sugar	3.8	65
	69.6	424

Lunch		
Rice and Tomato Soup*	56.6	214
Mushroom Omelet*	73.8	127
2 oz. lettuce and ½ tomato	8.4	14
Apple Sauce Supreme*	30.7	86
1 sl. Low-Sodium Bread	3.5	97
1 t. butter	.2	38
Coffee†—2 t. cream and 1 t. sugar	3.8	65
	177.0	641

Dinner		
½ grapefruit with 1 t. honey	2.3	39
Beef Stew* (⅔ of recipe for today, ⅓ for tomorrow lunch)	151.4	386
1 sl. Low-Sodium Bread	3.5	97
Endive salad—¼ small head	2.6	1
1 T. French Dressing (see Menu 3)	—	88
Apple Pie*—⅛ slice	2.9	388
Coffee†—1 t. sugar and 2 t. cream	3.8	65
	166.5	1064
Total for Day	413.1	2129

* Asterisks denote dishes for which recipes are given.
† Decaffeinated coffee may be chosen. It contains 1.7 mg. sodium and 2 calories per cup. With 2 t. milk and 1 t. sugar added, one cup contains 6.5 mg. sodium and 27 calories.

RECIPES FOR MENU 4

Rice and Tomato Soup

Makes 2 servings.

	Milligrams Sodium	Calories
¼ cup rice (2⅔ ozs.)	4.8	272
½ cup tomatoes (unsalted)	20.4	24
½ t. butter	.1	19
¾ cup milk	87.8	114
	113.1	429

One portion equals 56.6 mg. sodium and 214 calories

Boil 4 cups of water. Wash rice and throw into boiling water. Boil until rice is soft, about 1 hour. Then boil tomatoes separately and rub them through strainer. Combine with rice. Add butter and milk and simmer a while.

Mushroom Omelet

1 egg	67.0	77
1 t. butter	.2	38
¼ onion (½ oz.)	1.4	4
1 T. green pepper (½ oz.)	—	4
2 oz. mushrooms	5.2	4
	73.8	127

Saute onion, mushrooms and green pepper in butter. When almost done add beaten egg and fry.

Apple Sauce Supreme

(Suggest making it in quantity large enough for 6 servings.)

8 t. milk	19.2	24
⅙ egg	11.3	13
1 t. sugar	—	19
⅓ cup apple sauce, canned (3 oz.)	.2	30
Few grains cinnamon	—	—
10 drops vanilla extract	—	—
Nutmeg	—	—
	30.7	86

Scald milk. Beat egg slightly. Add sugar, cinnamon to egg. Add hot milk to egg slowly, stirring constantly. Cook over hot water, stirring constantly until mixture coats a spoon. Remove. Add vanilla. Chill. Fold this sauce and apple sauce together. Serve in sherbets, sprinkled with nutmeg on top.

Beef Stew

(Enough for dinner and lunch tomorrow.)

	Milligrams Sodium	Calories
½ lb. beef	156.8	400
½ T. vegetable oil (Crisco)	—	55
1 potato	8.0	96
Bit of green pepper	—	—
1 medium onion (2 oz.)	5.8	14
1 carrot (2 oz.)	54.0	12
1 T. juice from tomatoes (canned, unsalted)	2.5	3
Few grains pepper	—	—
Few grains sugar	—	—
	227.1	580

⅔ for dinner equals 151.4 mg. sodium and 386 calories

Cut beef in cubes. Dredge with peppered flour. Brown on all sides in vegetable oil. Quarter potato, mince green pepper, peel onions, scrape carrots and cut in fourths lengthwise. Add to meat with remaining ingredients. Simmer 2 hours or until meat is tender. Thicken gravy with flour if desired.

Pastry for 2-Crust Pies

2 cups flour	5.4	900
¼ lb. butter	5.6	904
	11.0	1804

Sift flour. Cut in shortening until particles are the size of small peas. Sprinkle ½ T. cold water on mixture and mix in lightly with fork. Continue adding water in this fashion until the pastry gathers around the fork in a soft ball. Roll on lightly floured board to ⅛" thickness.

Apple Filling

1 lb. tart apples	9.6	160
1 cup sugar	.8	896
2 t. flour	.1	22
2 T. butter	1.4	226
Bit of nutmeg and cinnamon	—	—
	11.9	1304

Quarter apples and slice thin. Line 9" pie pan with pastry. Mix sugar, flour and spices. Rub a little of this into pastry. Arrange apples and add remaining mixture. Dot with butter. Place top crust on. Make slits. Bake in 400° oven 45 minutes.

MENU 5

Breakfast	Milligrams Sodium	Calories
8 oz. pineapple juice	2.2	144
1 cup Puffed Wheat (½ oz.)	.4	55
½ banana, cut in cereal (2 oz.)	.6	44
½ cup milk	58.0	76
1 Hot Roll*	8.0	77
1 t. butter	.2	38
Coffee†—2 t. cream and 1 t. sugar	3.8	65
	73.2	499

Lunch		
Beef Stew left over from yesterday's meal (see Menu 4)	76.0	193
1 Hot Roll*	8.0	77
1 t. butter	.2	38
Salad—½ orange, 2 oz. lettuce	8.0	22
4 oz. canned peaches (2 halves)	6.8	76
Coffee†—2 t. cream and 1 t. sugar	3.8	65
	102.8	471

Dinner		
8 oz. Breaded Veal Cutlet*	240.8	488
4 oz. Pan-Fried Potatoes*	8.0	316
4 oz. Brussels Sprouts*	9.0	69
Salad—½ oz. cucumber, 1 oz. lettuce, ½ tomato, ½ oz. green pepper	6.8	16
Custard Cake Pudding*	64.2	319
	328.8	1208
Total for Day	504.8	2178

* Asterisks denote dishes for which recipes are given.
† Decaffeinated coffee may be chosen. It contains 1.7 mg. sodium and 2 calories per cup. With 2 t. milk and 1 t. sugar added, one cup contains 6.5 mg. sodium and 27 calories.

RECIPES FOR MENU 5

Hot Rolls

Makes 12 rolls.

	Milligrams Sodium	Calories
½ yeast cake (½ oz.)	5	12
½ cup milk	58.0	76
½ cup flour	1.3	225
½ egg	33.3	38
7 T. flour	1.4	231
2 T. sugar	.1	112
2 T. melted butter	1.4	226
	96.0	920

One roll equals 8.0 mg. sodium and 77 calories

Scald milk, cool to lukewarm, and add to crumbled yeast cake. Stir until yeast is dissolved. Add flour. Let rise in warm place until light. Beat egg, stir into yeast mixture with sugar and shortening. Add enough flour to make stiff dough (about 7 T.). Spread with melted butter. Cover. Place in refrigerator overnight. Then rise until double. Roll ⅔" thick on lightly covered board. Cut with biscuit cutter 2" in diameter. Spread with melted butter. Fold over. Cover, let rise until double. Bake in hot oven 10 to 12 minutes.

Breaded Veal Cutlet

½ lb. veal cutlet
Bread crumbs
Beaten egg
Vegetable shortening

Total given by McCance and Widdowson	240.8	488

Wipe cutlets with damp cloth. Sprinkle with pepper. Dip in crumbs. Dip in beaten eggs and then in crumbs again. Saute slowly in melted fat until well-browned. Add some water, about 2 T., and cover. Simmer until thoroughly cooked.

Brussels Sprouts

	Milligrams Sodium	Calories
¼ lb. Brussels sprouts	8.8	20
1 t. butter	.2	38
1 t. flour	—	11
	9.0	69

Cook sprouts until tender. Then melt butter. Add flour and a little water from cooked sprouts. Pour over sprouts and serve.

Pan-Fried Potatoes

¼ lb. potatoes	8.0	96
2 T. vegetable shortening	—	220
	8.0	316

Slice potatoes thin. Soak in cold water for ½ hour. Dry. Heat oil and place slices in pan. Cover. Brown on both sides.

Custard Cake Pudding

¼ cup sugar	.2	224
½ T. flour	.1	16
¼ cup milk	29.0	38
¼ lemon	1.4	3
½ egg beaten separately	33.5	38
	64.2	319

Mix sugar and flour. Add milk to egg yolks, pour over sugar mixture and mix well. Then add beaten whites and juice and grated rind of lemon. Put in buttered dish, set in pan of hot water and bake 40 minutes in moderate oven. Turn out on serving dish when cold. Liquid in bottom of pan serves as sauce. You may serve with whipped cream.

MENU 6

Breakfast	Milligrams Sodium	Calories
8 oz. apricot nectar	4.0	136
¼ cup Instant Ralston (1 oz.) with	.2	110
½ cup milk with	58.0	76
2 T. raisins	7.5	35
1 t. butter	.2	38
1 sl. Low-Sodium Bread (see Menu 1)	3.5	97
Coffee†—2 t. cream and 1 t. sugar	3.8	65
	77.2	557

Lunch		
Spicy Creamed Egg*	106.5	225
1 boiled mashed potato	4.0	92
Stewed carrots*	55.8	91
Peach Cocktail*	6.0	99
Coffee†—2 t. cream and 1 t. sugar	3.8	65
	176.1	572

Dinner		
Lamb Curry with Rice*	163.3	609
¼ lb. green peas, cooked	—	56
2 oz. hearts of lettuce	6.8	6
4 t. Vinegar Dressing (see Menu 1)	3.0	63
Lemon Sponge Pudding*	53.8	226
Coffee†—2 t. cream and 1 t. sugar	3.8	65
	230.7	1025
Total for Day	484.0	2154

* Asterisks denote dishes for which recipes are given.
† Decaffeinated coffee may be chosen. It contains 1.7 mg. sodium and 2 calories per cup. With 2 t. milk and 1 t. sugar added, one cup contains 6.5 mg. sodium and 27 calories.

RECIPES FOR MENU 6

Spicy Creamed Eggs

(To be served with mashed potatoes.)

	Milligrams Sodium	Calories
1 egg, hardboiled	67.0	77
⅓ cup milk	39.0	50
2 t. butter	.4	76
2 t. flour	.1	22
Pinch of chili powder	—	—
Bit of minced onion	—	—
	106.5	225

Add flour and chili to melted butter and blend. Add milk, minced onion. Cook over hot water, stirring until thickened. Cut eggs in quarters and add. Serve with mashed potatoes.

Stewed Carrots

	Sodium	Calories
¼ medium onion (½ oz.)	1.4	3
2 t. butter	.4	76
1 medium sliced carrot (2 oz.)	54.0	12
Pepper	—	—
	55.8	91

Chop onion fine. Saute slowly in butter until tender. Add carrots and pepper. Cover and simmer over low heat for 30 min. Add some water if necessary.

Peach Cocktail

	Sodium	Calories
2 peaches (5 oz.)	4.0	55
½ T. honey	1.3	27
1 t. lemon juice	—	—
3 T. orange juice	.7	17
⅔ cup hot water	—	—
	6.0	99

Peel and stone the peaches. Mash them. Add honey and water. Stir and allow to cool. Then add juices of lemon and oranges. Serve chilled in sherbet glasses.

Lamb Curry

	Milligrams Sodium	Calories
5 oz. lean lamb (weighed without the bone)	157.0	265
½ onion, sliced thin (1 oz.)	1.5	3
2½ t. shortening (butter)	.5	95
½ t. curry	.5	3
1 T. flour	.2	33
1 cup hot boiled rice (6 oz.)	3.6	210
	163.3	609

Cut lamb into small cubes, removing all fat. Brown slightly. Brown onions until they are almost black and add to lamb. Add curry powder and boiling water, just enough to cover. Cover and simmer 2 hours or more until very tender. Add more water if necessary. When cooked, thicken sauce with flour. Have rice cooked very dry and serve the rice with curried lamb on top.

Lemon Sponge Pudding

Makes 2 servings.

	Sodium	Calories
1 egg, beaten separately	67.0	77
⅓ lemon rind and juice	1.7	4
⅓ cup sugar	.2	298
2 t. flour	.1	22
⅓ cup milk	38.6	50
	107.6	451

One portion equals 53.8 mg. sodium and 226 calories

Add grated rind and juice to egg yolks which have been beaten until thick and lemon colored. Add mixture of sugar and flour slowly. Beat egg whites until stiff enough to hold their shape and fold into the mixture. Pour into shallow dish. Set in pan of cold water and bake 45 minutes in moderate oven.

MENU 7

Breakfast	Milligrams Sodium	Calories
1 orange, sliced	2.4	32
1 cup Puffed Rice (½ oz.) with	.1	60
2 oz. blueberries with	.2	30
½ cup milk	58.0	76
1 sl. Low-Sodium Bread, toasted (see Menu 1)	3.5	97
1 t. butter	.2	38
1 T. marmalade	5.2	74
Coffee†—2 t. cream and 1 t. sugar	3.8	65
	73.4	472

Lunch		
Curried Egg and Mushrooms*	78.8	242
1 t. butter	.2	38
1 sl. Low-Sodium Bread	3.5	97
Vegetable salad—½ tomato, 1 oz. lettuce, 1 oz. green pepper, 1 oz. cucumber	8.8	22
½ cup milk	58.0	76
3 Seed Cookies*	12.0	255
	161.3	730

Dinner		
½ lb. Pan-Browned Pork Chops* with Creole	70.6	304
Sauce* (make 2 portions, one for tomorrow's lunch for the spaghetti)	5.0	20
1 baked sweet potato (4 oz.)	20.4	92
2½ oz. Candied Carrots*	68.1	62
½ oz. endive salad (¼ small head) with	2.6	1
4 t. Vinegar Dressing (see Menu 1)	3.0	63
Marmalade Tapioca*	96.2	323
	265.9	865
Total for Day	500.6	2067

* Asterisks denote dishes for which recipes are given.
† Decaffeinated coffee may be chosen. It contains 1.7 mg. sodium and 2 calories per cup. With 2 t. milk and 1 t. sugar added, one cup contains 6.5 mg. sodium and 27 calories.

RECIPES FOR MENU 7

Curried Egg and Mushrooms

(Serve on toast.)

	Milligrams Sodium	Calories
¼ t. curry powder	.2	1
2 T. cream	11.4	115
1 hard-cooked egg, chopped	67.0	77
1 t. chopped onion	—	—
1 t. butter	.2	38
1 t. flour	—	11
¼ cup water	—	—
	78.8	242

Cook onion and mushroom in fat until tender and slightly brown. Add flour and stir well. Add water gradually and cook until thick, stirring constantly. Add curry powder and simmer for 10 minutes. Add egg. Stir in cream and bring to boiling point. Serve at once on toast.

Seed Cookies

Makes 20 cookies.

½ cup sugar	.4	448
⅜ cup shortening, Crisco or butter	4.2	678
1 egg slightly beaten	67.0	77
4 t. brandy	.5	51
Grated rind of ½ lemon	1.7	4
1 cup flour	2.7	450
3 T. caraway seeds	3.0	—
	79.5	1708

One cookie equals 4.0 mg. sodium and 85 calories

Cream sugar and butter well. Add eggs, brandy, lemon rind and flour. Roll thin. Sprinkle with seeds. Roll again and cut in fancy shapes. Bake 15 minutes in 300° oven.

PAN-BROWNED PORK CHOPS AND CREOLE SAUCE

	Milligrams Sodium	Calories
½ lb. pork chops, lean, weighed with bone	70.6	304
Creole sauce for 2:		
½ onion chopped fine, 1 oz.	1.5	4
2 T. sweet red pepper, chopped fine	.1	8
2 T. green peppers, chopped fine	.1	8
½ T. parsley, ⅕ oz.	1.8	1
Bit of garlic	.5	1
2 mushrooms cut small, 1 oz.	2.6	2
1 tomato, peeled and cut	3.2	16
	9.8	40

Cook chops slowly for ½ hour. Add creole sauce. Put in baking dish and bake slowly for 1 hour to 1½ hours, basting at ½ hour intervals.

Sauce: Combine all ingredients and cook slowly for 1 hour.

Candied Carrots

2½ oz. carrots	68.0	15
10 drops lemon juice	—	—
½ T. sugar	—	28
2 t. water	—	—
½ t. butter	.1	19
	68.1	62

Clean carrots and cut lengthwise. Add all ingredients. Cover and cook over low heat until tender and glazed.

Marmalade Tapioca

Can best be made for 6 servings.

⅙ egg	11.0	13
⅔ cup milk	77.3	101
1 T. tapioca	.4	34
4 t. sugar	—	76
⅙ lemon	.6	1
4 t. orange marmalade	6.9	98
	96.2	323

Mix egg yolk with small amount of milk. Add tapioca, sugar and rest of milk. Cook over rapidly boiling water 10–12 minutes, stirring frequently. Beat egg white stiff. Fold hot mixture into egg white. Cool. Fold in lemon juice and rind and add ½ cup orange marmalade. Serve in sherbet glasses.

MENU 8

Breakfast	Milligrams Sodium	Calories
4 oz. grapefruit juice (unsweetened)	.4	40
2 T. farina, ⅔ oz. (Do not use the quick cooking type)	.1	67
½ cup milk	58.0	76
1 sl. Low-Sodium Bread (see Menu 1)	3.5	97
1 t. butter	.2	38
Coffee†—2 t. cream and 1 t. sugar	3.8	65
	66.0	383

Lunch		
1 scrambled egg	67.0	77
1 t. butter	.2	38
2 oz. spaghetti with	4.4	64
Creole Sauce (made for pork chops on Menu 7)	5.0	20
Salad—2 oz. lettuce and ½ sliced orange	8.0	22
2 Sugar Cookies*	.6	136
Coffee†—2 t. cream and 1 t. sugar	3.8	65
	89.0	422

Dinner		
Spanish Chicken*	193.3	630
French Fried Onions*	70.3	302
1 boiled potato, sprinkled with parsley	4.0	92
1 sl. Low-Sodium Bread	3.5	97
Salad—1 oz. cabbage and 1 oz. pineapple	6.9	20
Spicy Baked Apple*	2.1	152
Coffee†—2 t. cream and 1 t. sugar	3.8	65
	283.9	1358
Total for Day	438.9	2163

* Asterisks denote dishes for which recipes are given.
† Decaffeinated coffee may be chosen. It contains 1.7 mg. sodium and 2 calories per cup. With 2 t. milk and 1 t. sugar added, one cup contains 6.5 mg. sodium and 27 calories.

RECIPES FOR MENU 8

Sugar Cookies

Makes 2 dozen cookies.

	Milligrams Sodium	Calories
1 cup flour	2.7	450
¼ cup sugar	.2	224
½ cup butter	5.6	904
1 T. sugar	—	56
½ t. vanilla extract	—	—
	8.5	1634

One cookie equals .3 mg. sodium and 68 calories

Mix flour and sugar. Rub in shortening with fingertips. Form into long rolls; wrap in waxed paper. Chill until firm. Slice thin; place on baking sheet. Mix tablespoon sugar with vanilla. Sprinkle on cookies. Bake in moderately hot oven until slightly browned.

Spanish Chicken

¾ lb. frying chicken (weighed with bone)	146.4	348
⅞ cup canned tomatoes, unsalted (7 oz.)	35.7	42
⅛ t. sugar	—	—
¼ lb. mushrooms	10.4	8
½ cup cooked peas	.4	56
2 T. flour and pepper	.4	66
1 T. cooking oil (vegetable oils)	—	110
	193.3	630

Wipe chicken well and dredge in flour seasoned with pepper. Brown in small quantity of oil. Add tomatoes and sugar. Cover. Simmer ½ hour or until tender. Add cleaned mushrooms to chicken. Add cooked peas. Heat 10 minutes and serve.

French Fried Onions

2 medium onions (4 oz.)	11.6	28
½ cup milk	58.5	76
1½ T. salad oil	—	165
1 T. flour	.2	33
	70.3	302

Soak onion rings in milk about 10 minutes. Dip in flour and fry in heated fat until brown. Drain.

Spicy Baked Apple

	Milligrams Sodium	Calories
1 apple	2.0	40
4 t. water	—	—
2 whole cloves	—	—
2 T. sugar	.1	112
Small bit of stick cinnamon	—	—
	2.1	152

Wash and core apple. Place piece of cinnamon in center. Stick with cloves and place in pan. Add water, cover. Bake in moderate oven 30 minutes until tender but not soft. Remove. Combine liquid from pan with sugar. Boil 1 minute. Baste apples with syrup and place under broiler to glaze tops.

MENU 9

Breakfast	Milligrams Sodium	Calories
½ grapefruit	.8	12
¼ cup Maltex—wheat cereal (1 oz.)	1.0	110
½ cup milk	58.0	76
1 Hot Roll (see Menu 5)	8.0	77
1 t. butter	.2	38
Coffee†—2 t. cream and 1 t. sugar	3.8	65
	71.8	378

Lunch		
Strained Vegetable Soup*	62.3	133
French Omelet*	67.2	115
Salad—1 oz. cucumber, 1 oz. lettuce, ½ tomato	8.0	14
1 T. French Dressing (see Menu 3)	—	88
1 roll and 1 t. butter	8.2	115
Coffee†—2 t. cream and 1 t. sugar	3.8	65
	149.5	530

Dinner		
Baked Cod in Milk*	229.7	394
1 boiled potato	4.0	92
Fried Eggplant*	5.8	138
1 roll	8.0	77
Tropical Pudding*	9.0	245
Coffee†—2 t. cream and 1 t. sugar	3.8	65
	260.3	1011
Total for Day	481.6	1919

* Asterisks denote dishes for which recipes are given.
† Decaffeinated coffee may be chosen. It contains 1.7 mg. sodium and 2 calories per cup. With 2 t. milk and 1 t. sugar added, one cup contains 6.5 mg. sodium and 27 calories.

RECIPES FOR MENU 9

Strained Vegetable Soup

Makes 3 servings.

	Milligrams Sodium	Calories
1 carrot (2 oz.)	54.0	12
1 onion (2 oz.)	5.8	14
1 potato (4 oz.)	8.0	96
1 tomato (3 oz.)	2.4	12
1 T. butter	.7	113
1 cup milk	116.1	152
Pepper	—	—
	187.0	399

One serving equals 62.3 mg. sodium and 133 calories

Cut up vegetables. Put up in enough water to cover and boil until potato and carrot are soft. Then pour through soup strainer and mash vegetables fine. Add butter, milk and pepper. Allow to simmer.

French Omelet

1 t. butter	.2	38
1 egg	67.0	77
1 T. water	—	—
Pepper	—	—
	67.2	115

Add water and pepper to well beaten egg. Pour into melted butter in frying pan and cook over low heat until the egg is done at bottom. Tilt and allow uncooked portions to flow to bottom. Repeat until egg is cooked throughout. Fold and serve.

Baked Cod in Milk

½ lb. cod	136.0	192
3 T. cream	17.1	172
3 T. water	—	—
2 T. fine bread crumbs	76.6	30
Pepper	—	—
Chopped chives or scallions as garnish	—	—
	229.7	394

Place fish steaks in greased baking dish. Preheat oven to moderate temperature. Mix cream with water and pour over fish and bake uncovered for 25 minutes to ½ hour. Add bread crumbs and pepper; sprinkle over carefully. Return to oven until crumbs have absorbed some of the sauce. Serve with chopped chives or scallions as a garnish.

FRIED EGGPLANT

	Milligrams Sodium	Calories
8 oz. eggplant	5.6	32
2 t. vegetable shortening	—	73
1 T. flour	.2	33
Pepper	—	—
	5.8	138

Pare eggplant and cut in thin slices. Pepper. Dip in flour and cook slowly in oil until they turn brown on both sides.

TROPICAL PUDDING

	Milligrams Sodium	Calories
⅓ banana	.4	22
3 T. canned pineapple (1 oz.)	.3	18
3 T. sliced strawberries	1.0	10
⅓ cup cooked rice (2¼ oz.)	1.3	79
4 t. heavy cream	6.0	80
2 t. powdered sugar	—	36
1 whole strawberry	—	—
	9.0	245

Cut banana; combine with pineapple and strawberries. Add fruits to rice. Whip cream, add powdered sugar, fold into rice and fruit mixture. Serve in glasses with whole strawberry.

MENU 10

Breakfast	Milligrams Sodium	Calories
4 oz. canned pears (2 halves)	9.2	72
¼ cup Wheatena (1 oz.)	.2	110
½ cup milk (hot) spiced with	58.0	76
1 t. sugar and bit of cinnamon	—	19
1 Hot Roll (see Menu 5)	8.0	77
2 t. butter	.4	76
Coffee†—2 t. cream and 1 t. sugar	3.8	65
	79.6	495

Lunch		
Sliced hard-boiled eggs on 2 oz. of lettuce	73.8	83
Cucumbers in Sour Cream*	15.6	119
2 Sugar Cookies (see Menu 8)	.6	136
Coffee†—2 t. cream and 1 t. sugar	3.8	65
	93.8	403

Dinner		
8 oz. steak, broiled	156.8	400
1 baked potato and 1 t. butter	8.2	134
¼ lb. buttered string beans, 1 t. butter	3.8	46
Salad—½ apple, ½ grapefruit slices on lettuce leaf	5.4	35
1 T. French Dressing (see Menu 3)	—	88
2½ oz. ice cream	71.2	145
Coffee†—2 t. cream and 1 t. sugar	3.8	65
	249.2	913
Total for Day	422.6	1811

* Asterisks denote dishes for which recipes are given.
† Decaffeinated coffee may be chosen. It contains 1.7 mg. sodium and 2 calories per cup. With 2 t. milk and 1 t. sugar added, one cup contains 6.5 mg. sodium and 27 calories.

RECIPE FOR MENU 10

Cucumbers in Sour Cream

	Milligrams Sodium	Calories
¼ medium cucumber	1.8	1
¼ medium onion	1.4	3
2 T. sour cream	11.4	115
1 t. vinegar	1.0	—
Bit of sugar, dry mustard, black pepper, garlic	—	—
	15.6	119

Slice cucumber and onion thin. Rub dish with garlic. Place onion on bottom, cucumber on top, in layers. Cover mixture with remaining ingredients blended into a dressing. Cover and chill before serving.

MENU 11

Breakfast	Milligrams Sodium	Calories
8 oz. pineapple juice	2.2	144
French Toast Vanilla* (2 pieces)	84.6	414
1 t. unsalted butter	.2	38
Hot herb tea (without caffeine) or	—	—
Decaffeinated coffee—2 t. milk and 1 t. sugar	6.5	27
	93.5	623

Lunch		
1 hard-boiled egg, sliced with paprika sprinkled on it	67.0	77
1⅓ cup Italian Potato and Zucchini Salad*	45.3	243
1 slice Herb Toast* with	3.7	135
1 T. Parmesan cheese, grated	38.0	20
Hot herb tea (without caffeine)	—	—
	154.0	475

Dinner		
Chicken and Red Grapes* (1 piece of chicken)	130.1	284
4 asparagus spears, steamed	2.3	20
Sweet Potatoes 'n' Apples* (1 serving)	30.0	177
¼ cup raw brown rice, boiled (If white rice is used, sodium count is 4.2 mg. for ¼ cup raw)	2.8	167
1 Hot Roll (see Menu 5)	8.0	77
1 t. unsalted butter	.2	38
Decaffeinated coffee—2 t. milk and 1 t. sugar	6.5	27
	179.9	790
Total for Day	427.4	1888

* Asterisks denote dishes for which recipes are given.

RECIPES FOR MENU 11

French Toast Vanilla

	Milligrams Sodium	Calories
1 T. unsalted butter	1.0	105
1 egg, beaten	67.0	77
2 sl. Low-Sodium Bread (see Menu 1)	7.0	194
2 T. milk	15.9	5
¼ t. vanilla extract	—	—
1/16 t. nutmeg	—	—
1 T. apple butter, unsweetened	—	33
	90.9	414

Beat egg slightly and add the milk, vanilla and nutmeg. Dip the bread into the mixture. Heat butter and brown on each side about 3 minutes per side. (Use nonstick cookware when possible to cut down on butter and calorie count.) Serve with unsweetened apple butter as desired.

Italian Potato and Zucchini Salad

Makes 3 servings.

2 cups cooked potatoes, peeled and diced	127.9	237
1½ cups sliced zucchini	2.0	37
½ cup tomatoes	2.7	13
1/8 cup onion	2.0	5
1/6 cup olive oil	—	335
2 T. or 1/8 cup pine nuts	.8	102
1 T. lemon juice	.3	1
1 t. fresh parsley	—	—
¼ t. dry basil	.1	—
Few sprinkles oregano	—	—
Few sprinkles black pepper	—	—
	135.8	730

One 1⅓-cup serving equals 45.3 mg. sodium and 243 calories

Combine potatoes, zucchini, tomato and onion. Mix together the olive oil and herbs. Pour over vegetables. Toss and chill. Add the pine nuts when ready to serve.

Herb Toast

1 sl. Low-Sodium Bread (see Menu 1)	3.5	97
1 t. unsalted butter	.2	38
Sprinkle basil, oregano, rosemary and thyme	—	—
	3.7	135

Butter bread. Sprinkle herbs on bread and toast in toaster oven or bake in a 400° oven.

Chicken and Red Grapes

Makes 2 servings.

	Milligrams Sodium	Calories
2 chicken breasts skinned (about ¾ lb.)	244.8	394
1 T. flour	.2	30
¼ t. basil	.1	—
¼ t. tarragon	.3	—
¼ t. paprika	.1	—
Sprinkle black pepper	—	—
1 clove garlic	1.7	4
1½ t. olive oil	—	66
2 T. water	—	—
¼ cup white wine	12.2	44
½ cup seedless grapes	.9	29
½ t. lemon juice	.1	—
	260.4	567

One chicken breast equals 130.2 mg. sodium and 284 calories

Shake chicken in brown bag filled with the flour, basil, tarragon, paprika and pepper. Brown the chicken in oil and 2 T. water in a nonstick frying pan. Remove the chicken. Saute the garlic. Return the chicken to pan and add the wine. Bring to boil, cover and simmer for 15 minutes. Add lemon juice, grapes and ¼ cup of water and cook for 5 minutes. Remove chicken and grapes. Cook lemon juice and water and wine combination until it is reduced by half to be used as sauce.

Sweet Potatoes 'n' Apples

Makes 3 servings.

3 medium-size sweet potatoes	86.3	413
1 medium apple, thinly sliced (about 1 cup)	2.2	41
2 T. lemon juice	.6	2
2 t. unsalted butter	.6	76
¼ t. cinnamon	.2	—
	89.9	532

One sweet potato equals 30 mg. sodium and 177 calories

Boil sweet potatoes with skins on for 25 minutes. Peel and cut them into ½″ slices. Steam or boil the thinly sliced apple. Preheat oven to 350°. Layer apples and sweet potatoes in baking dish, sprinkling lemon juice and cinnamon and dotting butter between layers. Pour the water in which apples were boiled over the top and bake 30 minutes.

MENU 12

Breakfast	Milligrams Sodium	Calories
Strawberry Yogurt Shake*	174.9	172
½ cup Great Grain and Nut Cereal*	47.2	314
¼ cup low-fat milk	37.5	36
Herb tea (without caffeine)	—	—
	259.6	522

Lunch		
1 cup Pasta e Fagioli*	18.9	316
1 sl. Herb Toast (see Menu 11)	3.7	135
Garden Salad*	23.1	17
2 T. Tarragon Vinegar*	6.2	1
Decaffeinated coffee—2 t. milk and 1 t. sugar	6.5	27
	58.4	496

Dinner		
Halibut Kabobs*	103.9	316
¼ cup or 4 T. raw long-grain brown rice, boiled	2.8	167
1 t. unsalted butter	.2	38
Bermuda Tomato Salad*	5.1	108
3 small stalks broccoli (about 6 oz.)	40.8	78
1 T. lemon juice	.3	1
1 Hot Roll (see Menu 5)	8.0	77
Herb tea (without caffeine)	—	—
	161.1	785
Total for Day	479.1	1803

* Asterisks denote dishes for which recipes are given.

RECIPES FOR MENU 12

Strawberry Yogurt Shake

	Milligrams Sodium	Calories
8 oz. plain low-fat yogurt	172.5	118
1 t. honey (if desired)	.9	20
½ cup fresh or frozen unsweetened strawberries	1.5	34
	174.9	172

Mix yogurt, honey and strawberries in the blender.

Great Grain and Nut Cereal

Makes 6 cups.

	Sodium	Calories
1½ cups oats	40.1	487
1½ cups wheat flakes	453.8	175
½ cup heated vegetable oil	—	980
½ cup unsalted hulled sunflower seeds	22.0	406
½ cup unsalted sesame seeds	—	437
½ cup unsalted walnuts	1.4	276
½ cup unsalted almonds, chopped	4.3	401
½ cup chopped dates	4.5	221
¼ cup dried apricots	18.2	59
¼ cup raisins	21.5	101
½ cup wheat germ	1.0	216
1 T. vanilla extract	.1	6
	566.9	3765

One ½-cup serving equals 47.2 mg. sodium and 314 calories

Preheat oven to 300°. Toast the oats and wheat flakes mixed with the heated vegetable oil for 15 minutes, stirring frequently. Then add the seeds, nuts and vanilla extract and toast 10 more minutes, stirring and shaking often. Remove from oven and add the chopped dates, dried apricots, raisins and wheat germ. Store in the refrigerator. Serve with milk.

Pasta e Fagioli

Makes 3 servings.

	Milligrams Sodium	Calories
3 cups water	—	—
½ cup dried navy beans	.7	270
3 T. olive oil	—	396
2 cloves garlic	3.4	8
2 T. unsalted tomato paste	21.5	28
1 cup chopped onion	16.0	37
1 cup uncooked shell macaroni (about 2 oz.)	14.8	210
½ t. oregano	.2	—
½ t. basil	.2	—
Freshly ground black pepper	—	—
	56.8	949

One 1-cup serving equals 18.9 mg. sodium and 316 calories

Soak the beans overnight in 3 cups water in the refrigerator. The following day, cook them for 2½ to 3 hours with 1 whole garlic clove and 1 T. olive oil. After the first hour of cooking, add the onions. During the last ½ hour of cooking mince the second garlic clove and saute it slowly with the herbs. Add this mixture and the unsalted tomato paste to the beans. Cook the mixture for the remaining ½ hour. Meanwhile, boil the macaroni; drain and mix with beans. Add pepper to taste.

Garden Salad

1½ cups Romaine lettuce leaves, torn (about 11 medium leaves or 5 large ones)	7.4	10
¼ cup sliced mushrooms	1.6	2
2 T. shredded carrot	13.1	3
1 T. chopped Bermuda onion	1.0	2
	23.1	17

Mix all ingredients.

Tarragon Vinegar

Makes 1 pint (2 cups).

16 fl. oz. white wine vinegar (1 pint)	96.0	19
1 T. dried tarragon	3.0	—
	99.0	19

One tablespoon equals 3.1 mg. sodium

Add dried tarragon to white wine vinegar. Let stand before using.

Halibut Kabobs

Makes 2 servings.

	Milligrams Sodium	Calories
½ lb. halibut steak (with skin and bones removed)	190.7	209
¼ cup onions, cut into chunks	4.0	9
¼ cup tomato, cut into chunks	1.4	6
¼ cup green peppers, cut into chunks	.8	6
3 T. olive oil	—	396
3 T. white wine vinegar	9.0	2
1 clove garlic	1.7	4
¼ t. basil	.1	—
Sprinkle pepper	—	—
	207.7	632

One ¼-lb. serving equals 103.9 mg. sodium and 316 calories

Cut halibut into 1″ chunks. Marinate halibut steak in olive oil, vinegar and herb mixture for 5 minutes. Remove from marinade and put on skewers. Cut onion, tomato and green pepper into chunks. Steam the green pepper and onion until tender. Then alternate onion, tomato and green pepper on another skewer. Barbecue for a total of 10 minutes, turning as needed, brushing marinade mixture on both sides. Place vegetable skewer on the side of grill where heat is least intense.

You may also broil kabobs in oven: Place skewers 3″ from the heat for 10 minutes, basting and turning frequently.

Bermuda Tomato Salad

1 medium tomato, sliced	3.7	17
3 thin slices Bermuda onion	1.4	3
2 t. olive oil	—	88
Sprinkle pepper	—	—
Sprinkle basil and oregano	—	—
	5.1	108

Mix tomato and onion. Pour oil over and sprinkle with pepper and herbs. Serve at room temperature.

MENUS 13–24

900–1000 Milligrams of Sodium
1800–2200 Calories

MENU 13

Breakfast	Milligrams Sodium	Calories
4 oz. strawberries with	1.6	28
1 t. sugar with	—	19
3 T. cream	17.1	174
1 poached egg	67.0	77
1 sl. whole wheat bread (toasted)	123.0	70
1 t. butter	.2	38
Coffee†—2 t. cream and 1 t. sugar	3.8	65
	212.7	471

Lunch		
1 plate Strained Vegetable Soup (see Menu 9)	62.3	133
1 lamb chop, broiled (3⅓ oz.)	104.6	176
4 oz. green peas, buttered, 1 t. butter	.6	94
1 sl. whole wheat bread	123.0	70
2 oz. shredded lettuce	6.8	6
1 T. French Dressing (see Menu 3)	—	88
Coffee†—2 t. cream and 1 t. sugar	3.8	65
2 Tea Cookies*	7.4	154
	308.5	786

Dinner		
½ lb. Breaded Veal Cutlets (see Menu 5)	240.8	488
Stewed Tomatoes*	73.2	129
1 baked potato	8.0	96
1 sl. whole wheat bread	123.0	70
Salad—½ apple, ½ grapefruit slices on lettuce leaf	5.4	35
4. oz. fruit salad, canned	10.0	80
	460.4	898
Total for Day	981.6	2155

* Asterisks denote dishes for which recipes are given.
† Decaffeinated coffee may be chosen. It contains 1.7 mg. sodium and 2 calories per cup. With 2 t. milk and 1 t. sugar added, one cup contains 6.5 mg. sodium and 27 calories.

RECIPES FOR MENU 13

Tea Cookies

Makes 10 cookies.

	Milligrams Sodium	Calories
3 T. shortening, Crisco, or butter	2.1	339
3 T. sugar	.1	168
½ egg	33.5	38
10 drops vanilla extract	—	—
½ cup flour	1.4	225
	37.1	770

One cookie equals 3.7 mg. sodium and 77 calories

Cream shortening. Add sugar gradually. Add egg, beating it in gradually. Add vanilla. Add flour slowly. Stir until smooth. Drop by teaspoon on greased baking sheet. Flatten them and bake in oven 10 minutes.

Stewed Tomatoes

1 T. minced onion (½ oz.)	1.4	3
1 t. butter	.2	38
½ cup tomatoes, canned, unsalted	20.4	24
4 t. bread crumbs	51.0	20
1 t. browned butter	.2	38
Bit of bay leaf	—	—
Bit of pepper	—	—
⅓ t. sugar	—	6
½ clove	—	—
	73.2	129

Chop onion fine. Cook in butter until slightly browned. Add tomatoes, bay leaf, pepper, sugar and clove. Cover. Cook 10 minutes. Remove bay leaf and cloves. Toss bread crumbs in browned butter. Add to tomatoes; mix well.

MENU 14

Breakfast	Milligrams Sodium	Calories
4 oz. stewed prunes (4 prunes)	3.4	120
¼ cup oatmeal (1 oz.)	9.5	115
½ cup milk	58.0	76
1 sl. whole wheat toast	123.0	70
1 t. butter	.2	38
1 T. orange marmalade	5.2	74
Coffee†—2 t. cream and 1 t. sugar	3.8	65
	203.1	558

Lunch		
Spring Vegetable Soup*	20.0	106
Mushroom Omelet (see Menu 4)	73.8	127
1 sl. whole wheat bread	123.0	70
1 t. butter	.2	38
2 Tea Cookies (see Menu 13)	7.4	154
Coffee†—2 t. cream and 1 t. sugar	3.8	65
	228.2	560

Dinner		
½ grapefruit and 1 t. honey	2.3	39
Macaroni with Liver*	79.6	231
Stewed Carrots (see Menu 6)	55.8	91
1 sl. whole wheat bread	123.0	70
1 t. butter	.2	38
3 oz. celery hearts (about 2)	116.7	9
2½ oz. ice cream	71.2	145
2 Tea Cookies (see Menu 13)	7.4	154
Coffee†—2 t. cream and 1 t. sugar	3.8	65
	460.0	842
Total for Day	891.3	1960

* Asterisks denote dishes for which recipes are given.
† Decaffeinated coffee may be chosen. It contains 1.7 mg. sodium and 2 calories per cup. With 2 t. milk and 1 t. sugar added, one cup contains 6.5 mg. sodium and 27 calories.

RECIPES FOR MENU 14

Spring Vegetable Soup

	Milligrams Sodium	Calories
1 leek (¼ oz.)	2.5	2
⅓ cup shelled peas (1⅔ oz.)	.4	30
⅓ cup asparagus tips, raw (2 oz.)	1.0	10
⅓ pint water	—	—
½ T. butter	.3	57
3 T. string beans (1 oz.)	1.8	4
⅙ carrot (½ oz.)	14.0	3
Pepper	—	—
	20.0	106

Heat butter in pot. Add white part of leek cut up small, peas, carrot cut up small, asparagus tips cut up, and finely cubed string beans. Simmer gently 5 minutes, covered. Then add water and pepper and cook 20 minutes.

Macaroni with Liver

2 oz. elbow macaroni	4.4	64
3 oz. sliced liver	73.2	123
1 t. shortening (butter)	.2	38
Bit of chopped onion	.8	2
Bit of crushed garlic	.2	—
2 t. boiling water	—	—
Slice of tomato, diced (1 oz.)	.8	4
	79.6	231

Dice liver. Heat fat in heavy skillet and put in liver, onion and garlic. Saute until tender and brown. Add tomato and pepper and boiling water and cook 10 minutes. Have macaroni freshly boiled and drained. Turn into hot serving dish, add liver, mix well, and serve at once.

MENU 15

Breakfast	Milligrams Sodium	Calories
8 oz. orange juice	4.0	88
Puffy Omelet*	69.0	114
1 sl. whole wheat toast	123.0	70
1 t. butter	.2	38
Coffee†—2 t. cream and 1 t. sugar	3.8	65
	200.0	375

Lunch		
4 oz. Sauteed Mushrooms* on	16.6	98
1 sl. whole wheat toast	123.0	70
1 t. butter	.2	38
Salad—½ orange and 2 oz. lettuce	8.0	22
2 Macaroons*	53.3	289
Coffee†—2 t. cream and 1 t. sugar	3.8	65
	204.9	582

Dinner		
Meat Loaf*	255.1	297
1 boiled parsley potato	4.0	92
Peas and Corn with Curry*	246.5	143
Apple Salad* and	14.6	88
1 T. French Dressing (see Menu 3)	—	88
Fruit Cup with Grenadine*	5.7	125
Coffee†—2 t. cream and 1 t. sugar	3.8	65
	529.7	898
Total for Day	934.6	1855

* Asterisks denote dishes for which recipes are given.
† Decaffeinated coffee may be chosen. It contains 1.7 mg. sodium and 2 calories per cup. With 2 t. milk and 1 t. sugar added, one cup contains 6.5 mg. sodium and 27 calories.

RECIPES FOR MENU 15

Puffy Omelet

	Milligrams Sodium	Calories
1 egg, separated	67.0	77
1 T. water	—	—
Few grains paprika	2.0	—
Few grains pepper	—	—
1 t. salad oil	—	37
	69.0	114

Add water, paprika and pepper to beaten egg yolk. Beat egg white. Fold yolk into egg white lightly. Heat salad oil in pan until all pan is coated. Pour mixture into pan and spread evenly. Cook over low heat until omelet is puffed and brown on bottom. Then set in moderate oven 5 minutes until top is firm to touch. Fold and turn on hot plate.

Sauteed Mushrooms

4 oz. mushrooms	10.4	8
1 small onion	5.8	14
2 t. butter	.4	76
Few grains pepper	—	—
	16.6	98

Cut up an onion and saute in butter. Place washed and cut up mushrooms into onion when it is light brown. Allow to simmer. Add pepper. Serve on toast.

Macaroons

Makes 2 macaroons.

(Suggest making about 4 times the recipe.)

4 t. sweetened condensed milk (1⅑ oz.)	45.2	111
⅓ cup moist coconut (1 oz.)	8.1	178
5 drops vanilla extract	—	—
3 drops almond extract	—	—
	53.3	289

Combine condensed milk and shredded coconut. Add vanilla and almond extracts. Drop by spoonfuls on greased baking sheet. Bake in moderate oven 10 minutes or until brown.

Meat Loaf

	Milligrams Sodium	Calories
½ cup tomatoes, canned, unsalted (4 oz.)	20.4	24
4 oz. ground beef	78.4	200
¼ cup bread crumbs	143.7	56
⅙ egg	11.1	13
1 T. onion (½ oz.)	1.5	4
	255.1	297

Drain tomatoes. Add pulp to ground meat. Add crumbs and pepper. Beat egg; add. Mince onion and add. Mix thoroughly. Grease pan and pack meat in. Bake in hot oven 45 minutes.

Peas and Corn with Curry

⅓ cup canned drained green peas (2 oz.)	132.0	48
¼ cup canned whole kernel corn (2 oz.)	114.2	38
½ T. butter	.3	57
Bit of curry powder	—	—
	246.5	143

Combine peas and corn. Melt butter and add curry powder. Pour over vegetables and mix well. Heat and serve.

Apple Salad

½ cup crushed canned pineapple (3 oz.)	.8	54
½ cup shredded cabbage (2 oz.)	12.8	14
½ apple, chopped	1.0	20
	14.6	88

Drain syrup from pineapple. Mix pineapple, cabbage and apple. Add dressing.

Fruit Cup with Grenadine

1 cubed orange	2.4	32
1 cubed banana (small)	.8	52
2 T. pineapple bits	.2	11
Seeded grapes (1 oz.)	1.1	18
Grenadine syrup (½ oz.)	1.4	12
	5.7	125

Combine, chill and serve.

MENU 16

Breakfast	Milligrams Sodium	Calories
½ grapefruit, sliced (4 oz.)	.8	12
1 oz. Shredded Wheat—1 biscuit with	4.7	103
½ banana (3 oz.)	.9	66
½ cup milk	58.0	76
1 T. marmalade	5.2	74
Coffee†—2 t. cream and 1 t. sugar	3.8	65
	73.4	396

Lunch		
Baked Eggs in Sour Cream*	127.0	362
Salad—½ apple, ½ grapefruit on lettuce	5.4	35
1 sl. whole wheat bread	123.0	70
1 t. butter	.2	38
Coffee†—2 t. cream and 1 t. sugar	3.8	65
	259.4	570

Dinner		
Baked Chicken*	216.7	509
Green Beans Creole*	216.9	163
1 mashed potato	4.0	92
2 oz. hearts of lettuce	6.8	6
Early American Pudding*	102.3	264
Coffee†—2 t. cream and 1 t. sugar	3.8	65
	550.5	1099
Total for Day	883.3	2065

* Asterisks denote dishes for which recipes are given.
† Decaffeinated coffee may be chosen. It contains 1.7 mg. sodium and 2 calories per cup. With 2 t. milk and 1 t. sugar added, one cup contains 6.5 mg. sodium and 27 calories.

RECIPES FOR MENU 16

Baked Eggs in Sour Cream

	Milligrams Sodium	Calories
3 T. chopped onions (1½ oz.)	4.3	11
½ T. shortening (butter)	.3	57
1 egg	67.0	77
3 T. sour cream	17.1	172
1 T. buttered soft crumbs	38.3	45
Pepper	—	—
	127.0	362

Cook onion until tender in butter. Spread this mixture on bottom of shallow, well-buttered casserole. Drop eggs on top of this and sprinkle with pepper. Bake in moderate oven 5 minutes. Remove and spread sour cream over eggs gently. Sprinkle with buttered crumbs. Return to oven for 10 minutes longer or until eggs are of the desired firmness.

Baked Chicken

	Milligrams Sodium	Calories
½ lb. breast meat (not weighed with rest of chicken)	177.6	368
Bit of pepper	—	—
1 T. flour	.2	33
⅓ cup milk	38.6	51
½ T. butter	.3	57
	216.7	509

Wash and dry chicken. Dust with peppered flour and place in roaster. Pour milk into roaster. Dot chicken with butter. Bake in hot oven 15 minutes. Reduce heat and bake for 1 hour longer. Baste chicken occasionally with milk in pan.

Green Beans Creole

	Milligrams Sodium	Calories
1 T. onion	1.4	4
1 t. salad oil	—	37
⅓ cup bread crumbs	191.4	75
½ cup canned tomatoes (4⅓ oz.)	22.1	26
½ cup frozen green beans (3⅙ oz.)	2.0	21
Pepper and few grains sugar	—	—
	216.9	163

Saute onion in oil. Add half of bread crumbs. Then combine tomatoes, sugar and pepper. Cook green beans. Add liquid to tomatoes and cook until liquid is evaporated. Add green beans and place ½ mixture in bottom of casserole. Add remaining bread crumbs. Repeat and bake in hot oven.

Early American Pudding

	Milligrams Sodium	Calories
1 T. yellow cornmeal (½ oz.)	—	55
⅔ cup milk	77.0	101
4 t. molasses (1⅑ oz.)	25.3	89
½ t. butter	—	19
Bit of ginger	—	—
Bit of cinnamon	—	—
	102.3	264

Combine cornmeal and spices. Scald half the milk; add slowly, stirring constantly. Add molasses. Mix thoroughly. Add remaining cold milk. Stir well. Cook over hot water, stirring occasionally, until slightly thickened. Pour into greased baking dish. Dot with butter. Set in pan of warm water and bake in slow oven about 2 hours.

MENU 17

Breakfast	Milligrams Sodium	Calories
Baked apple with 1 t. sugar and cinnamon	2.4	59
2 t. cream	3.8	38
1 boiled egg	67.0	77
1 sl. whole wheat toast	123.0	70
1 t. butter	.2	38
Coffee†—2 t. cream and 1 t. sugar	3.8	65
	200.2	347

Lunch		
½ grapefruit (4 oz.) with 1 t. honey	2.3	39
Vegetable Plate*	17.2	277
1 sl. whole wheat bread	123.0	70
1 t. butter	.2	38
Chocolate Custard*	132.4	179
Coffee†—2 t. cream and 1 t. sugar	3.8	65
	278.9	668

Dinner		
Broiled Flounder*	146.0	159
1 baked potato with	8.0	96
1 t. butter	.2	38
Scalloped Spinach*	188.0	108
Stuffed Celery*	112.7	25
Sweet Pilau*	25.8	459
Coffee†—2 t. cream and 1 t. sugar	3.8	65
	484.5	950
Total for Day	963.6	1965

* Asterisks denote dishes for which recipes are given.
† Decaffeinated coffee may be chosen. It contains 1.7 mg. sodium and 2 calories per cup. With 2 t. milk and 1 t. sugar added, one cup contains 6.5 mg. sodium and 27 calories.

RECIPES FOR MENU 17

Vegetable Plate

	Milligrams Sodium	Calories
1 potato (4 oz.)	8.0	96
2 oz. mushrooms	5.2	4
2 oz. yellow turnips	2.8	28
2 oz. green peas	.5	36
1 T. butter	.7	113
	17.2	277

Bake potato, saute mushrooms, boil mashed yellow turnips and cook green peas. Serve.

Chocolate Custard

Makes 2 servings.

⅓ oz. unsweetened chocolate	.3	60
⅓ cup strong coffee	—	—
⅓ cup milk	39.0	51
½ egg	34.0	39
5 t. sugar	—	95
1 t. melted butter	.2	38
10 drops vanilla extract	—	—
⅓ cup bread crumbs	191.4	75
	264.9	358

One portion equals 132.4 mg. sodium and 179 calories

Melt chocolate over hot water. Add milk and strong coffee. Bring to a scalding point. Beat egg and add sugar. Pour milk mixture on egg mixture. Add melted butter and vanilla. Place crumbs in casserole and pour custard mixture on them. Set in pan of warm water. Bake in moderate oven until done, about 1 hour.

Broiled Flounder

½ lb. of flounder (weighed with bone and skin)	145.6	120
Pepper	—	—
Lemon juice (½ oz.)	.2	1
1 t. melted butter	.2	38
	146.0	159

Split, clean and dry the fish. Sprinkle with pepper and lemon juice. Place skin side down on greased broiler. Broil 10 minutes, then turn and brown skin. Serve with melted butter flavored with lemon juice.

Scalloped Spinach

	Milligrams Sodium	Calories
⅓ cup chopped cooked spinach (3⅓ oz.)	116.3	25
1 t. minced onion	—	—
Pepper	—	—
⅙ egg	11.1	13
4 t. milk	9.6	12
4 t. buttered bread crumbs (38 calories for butter)	51.0	58
	188.0	108

Combine spinach, onion and pepper. Beat egg slightly; combine with milk. Add to spinach. Top with buttered crumbs. Bake in oven until crumbs are brown.

Stuffed Celery

	Milligrams Sodium	Calories
2 outer stalks of celery (1⅓ oz.—about 7″ stalk)	51.8	4
4 t. cottage cheese	60.9	21
Bit of minced onion	—	—
Bit of chili powder	—	—
	112.7	25

Stuff celery stalk with cottage cheese and onion mixture. Sprinkle with bit of chili. Cut each stalk in small pieces and serve.

Sweet Pilau

	Milligrams Sodium	Calories
1 T. rice	1.2	68
½ T. butter	.3	57
6 T. pineapple juice (3 oz.)	.3	54
2 t. brown sugar	1.5	23
1 T. seedless raisins	5.0	23
1 T. chopped walnuts	.4	62
Ground nutmeg	—	—
3 T. cream	17.1	172
	25.8	459

Wash rice. Add boiling water to cover. Cover and let stand 10 minutes. Drain. Heat butter and add rice. Stir until rice is coated. Add pineapple juice. Cover and cook slowly until rice is tender (50 minutes). Combine brown sugar, raisins, walnuts and nutmeg. Add to rice. Stir until blended. Cool. Whip cream and fold in.

MENU 18

Breakfast	Milligrams Sodium	Calories
8 oz. orange and grapefruit juice	2.4	84
1 cup Puffed Rice (½ oz.) with	.1	60
½ cup milk with	58.0	76
2 T. blueberries	.1	15
1 sl. whole wheat toast	123.0	70
1 t. butter	.2	38
Coffee†—2 t. cream and 1 t. sugar	3.8	65
	187.6	408

Lunch		
Asparagus Omelet*	68.1	87
1 boiled potato	4.0	92
1 t. butter	.2	38
Salad—1 oz. cucumber, ½ tomato, 1 leaf lettuce	8.7	14
Pineapple and Cocoanut (see Menu 3)	3.4	123
1 sl. whole wheat bread	123.0	70
Coffee†—2 t. cream and 1 t. sugar	3.8	65
	211.2	489

Dinner		
½ grapefruit with 1 t. honey	2.3	39
8 oz. broiled sirloin steak	156.8	400
French fried potatoes (made with 1 potato and fried in 2 T. vegetable oil)	8.0	316
Carrot Surprise*	300.7	116
Salad—1 oz. green pepper, 1 oz. cucumber, ½ tomato and 1 leaf lettuce	8.3	22
Frozen Sherbet*	31.0	205
Coffee†—2 t. cream and 1 t. sugar	3.8	65
	510.9	1163
Total for Day	909.7	2060

* Asterisks denote dishes for which recipes are given.
† Decaffeinated coffee may be chosen. It contains 1.7 mg. sodium and 2 calories per cup. With 2 t. milk and 1 t. sugar added, one cup contains 6.5 mg. sodium and 27 calories.

RECIPES FOR MENU 18

Asparagus Omelet

	Milligrams Sodium	Calories
1 egg, separated	67.0	77
2 oz. cooked fresh asparagus	1.0	10
Dash pepper	—	—
Dash paprika	—	—
	68.0	87

Beat egg yolk. Add asparagus, pepper, paprika and mix. Beat white stiff and fold in. Cook in hot greased frying pan on low heat until bottom is browned. Place in moderate oven a few minutes to dry out top. Cut omelet part way through center, fold over and serve.

Carrot Surprise

²/₃ c. canned diced carrots (3¹/₃ oz.)	267.0	40
¹/₂ egg	33.5	38
1 t. melted butter	.2	38
Pepper	—	—
	300.7	116

Heat carrots, drain and mash. Beat egg. Add to carrots with pepper and butter. Pack in muffin pan. Set in pan of hot water and bake in moderate oven 20 minutes.

Frozen Sherbet

Makes 6 servings.

1 egg	67.0	77
1 cup sugar	.8	896
1 cup milk	116.0	152
1 T. lemon juice	.2	1
3 T. orange juice	.7	17
4 oz. banana, mashed	1.2	88
	185.9	1231

One portion equals 31.0 mg. sodium and 205 calories

Beat egg. Add sugar and milk. Then add the mashed bananas and orange and lemon juice. Freeze in refrigerator tray until mushy. At that point beat with a fork until creamy and smooth. Return to tray and refrigerate until ready to serve.

MENU 19

Breakfast	Milligrams Sodium	Calories
8 oz. pineapple juice	.8	144
¼ cup Wheatena (1 oz.) with	.2	110
½ cup milk with	58.0	76
2 stewed prunes (2 oz.)	1.7	60
1 sl. whole wheat toast	123.0	70
1 t. butter	.2	38
Coffee†—2 t. cream and 1 t. sugar	3.8	65
	187.7	563

Lunch		
Salmon Salad*	277.1	134
1 boiled potato	4.0	92
1 sl. whole wheat bread	123.0	70
1 t. butter	.2	38
Cantaloupe Gelatin Salad* with	17.4	73
French Dressing for Fruit Salad*	1.2	108
Coffee†—2 t. cream and 1 t. sugar	3.8	65
	426.7	580

Dinner		
Braised Veal Chops*	244.9	315
French Fried Onions*	20.6	208
1 boiled potato	4.0	92
Orange Raisin Slaw*	20.2	56
Apple Pie—⅛ piece (see Menu 4)	2.9	388
Coffee†—2 t. cream and 1 t. sugar	3.8	65
	296.4	1124
Total for Day	910.8	2267

* Asterisks denote dishes for which recipes are given.
† Decaffeinated coffee may be chosen. It contains 1.7 mg. sodium and 2 calories per cup. With 2 t. milk and 1 t. sugar added, one cup contains 6.5 mg. sodium and 27 calories.

RECIPES FOR MENU 19

Salmon Salad

	Milligrams Sodium	Calories
2 oz. salmon, canned	268.4	120
1 small onion (1½ oz.)	4.3	11
1 t. vinegar	1.0	—
1 large leaf lettuce	3.4	3
	277.1	134

Mix ingredients and serve on lettuce leaf.

Cantaloupe Gelatin Salad

½ t. unflavored gelatin	—	5
½ t. cold water	—	—
1 t. boiling water	—	—
⅓ cup ginger ale (2½ oz.)	6.0	28
1 t. sugar	—	19
½ cup cantaloupe balls (3 oz.)	11.4	21
Chicory	—	—
	17.4	73

Sprinkle gelatin in cold water. Add boiling water, stir until dissolved. Add ginger ale and sugar. Chill until syrupy. Fold in cantaloupe balls. Pour into mold which has been chilled. Chill until firm. Garnish with chicory.

French Dressing for Fruit Salad

1 t. vinegar	1.0	—
Pinch of mustard	—	—
⅛ t. sugar	—	3
2¼ t. vegetable oil (olive oil)	—	99
¼ t. honey	.2	6
	1.2	108

Mix all ingredients thoroughly.

Braised Veal Chops

	Milligrams Sodium	Calories
8 oz. veal shoulder chops	243.2	248
1 t. butter	.2	38
½ T. flour	.1	17
1 T. sherry	1.4	12
¼ clove garlic, sliced	—	—
	244.9	315

Wipe chops with clean damp cloth and dip in flour. Heat fat; brown chops quickly on both sides. Pour sherry or vinegar mixture over them. Place slivered garlic on top. Cover and simmer for 25 to 30 minutes, depending on thickness of chops. When serving, spoon liquid from pan over the chops.

French Fried Onions

	Milligrams Sodium	Calories
½ large Bermuda onion (2 oz.), cut in thick slices	5.8	14
2 T. milk	14.4	18
2 T. flour	.4	66
1 T. vegetable oil	—	110
	20.6	208

Separate onion rings. Soak in milk for 30 minutes. Dip in peppered flour and fry in hot fat.

Orange Raisin Slaw

	Milligrams Sodium	Calories
⅓ orange	.8	11
½ cup shredded cabbage (2 oz.)	12.8	14
1⅓ T. seedless raisins	6.6	31
	20.2	56

Combine peeled orange slices and shredded cabbage with raisins. French dressing may be added.

MENU 20

Breakfast	Milligrams Sodium	Calories
1 orange, sliced	2.4	32
Poached Egg in Cream*	72.7	134
1 sl. whole wheat toast	123.0	70
1 t. butter	.2	38
Coffee†—2 t. cream and 1 t. sugar	3.8	65
	202.1	339

Lunch		
4 oz. grapefruit juice	.4	40
Tuna and Potatoes, au Gratin*	323.8	334
2 oz. shredded lettuce	6.8	6
1 T. French Dressing (see Menu 3)	—	88
Banana and Grape Gelatin*	2.4	106
Coffee†—2 t. cream and 1 t. sugar	3.8	65
	337.2	639

Dinner		
Erin Stew*	263.7	425
Salad—1 oz. cucumber, ½ tomato and 1 oz. lettuce	8.7	14
1 T. French Dressing (see Menu 3)	—	88
4 oz. boiled string beans with 1 t. butter	3.8	46
Orange Rice Custard (see Menu 1)	30.6	409
Coffee†—2 t. cream and 1 t. sugar	3.8	65
	301.6	1047
Total for Day	849.9	2025

* Asterisks denote dishes for which recipes are given.
† Decaffeinated coffee may be chosen. It contains 1.7 mg. sodium and 2 calories per cup. With 2 t. milk and 1 t. sugar added, one cup contains 6.5 mg. sodium and 27 calories.

RECIPES FOR MENU 20

Poached Eggs and Cream

	Milligrams Sodium	Calories
1 egg	67.0	77
1 T. heavy cream	5.7	57
	72.7	134

Butter pan generously. Set over low heat. Put cream in pan, break egg and slip into pan. Move pan slowly with circular motion until egg is set.

Tuna and Potatoes, au Gratin

	Sodium	Calories
1 hot baked potato (4 oz.)	8.0	96
Bit of grated onion	—	—
1½ oz. canned tuna (¼ cup)	231.3	131
½ oz. grated American cheddar	77.1	60
1 T. milk	7.2	9
1 t. butter	.2	38
Pepper	—	—
	323.8	334

Scoop out baked potato and mash. Season with milk, pepper and butter. Add grated onion. Drain and flake tuna and add. Refill potato. Sprinkle tops with cheese. Bake in moderate oven about 15 minutes.

Banana and Grape Gelatin

	Sodium	Calories
1 t. gelatin (plain)	.7	10
1 T. cold water	—	—
¼ cup grape juice (2 oz.)	.5	36
½ T. sugar	—	28
¾ t. lemon juice	—	—
3 T. banana slices	.3	20
3 T. diced oranges	.9	12
	2.4	106

Sprinkle gelatin on cold water. Heat grape juice and pour over gelatin. Add sugar and lemon juice. Stir until dissolved. Chill until thickened. Fold in the fruit and chill until firm.

Erin Stew

	Milligrams Sodium	Calories
5 oz. top round beef	98.0	250
1 t. vegetable shortening	—	37
2 small onions (2½ oz.)	7.2	18
1 small carrot (2 oz.)	54.0	12
1 small potato (3 oz.)	6.0	72
⅓ cup canned peas (1½ oz.)	98.5	36
	263.7	425

Cut meat into cubes. Dredge in flour. Brown on all sides in fat. Peel onions. Add. Cut carrots in strips. Add. Cube potato and add. Simmer 2½ hours, adding water if necessary. Add peas, liquid and all. Simmer ½ hour longer.

MENU 21

Breakfast	Milligrams Sodium	Calories
4 oz. stewed prunes (4 prunes)	3.4	120
¼ cup Maltex Cereal (1 oz.) with	1.1	110
½ cup milk with	58.0	76
1 T. raisins (¼ oz.)	5.0	23
1 sl. whole wheat bread	123.0	70
1 t. butter	.2	38
Coffee†—2 t. cream and 1 t. sugar	3.8	65
	194.5	502

Lunch		
Spring Salad*	204.3	226
1 sl. whole wheat bread	123.0	70
1 t. butter	.2	38
Apple Pudding*	160.9	379
Coffee†—2 t. cream and 1 t. sugar	3.8	65
	492.2	778

Dinner		
Sweet and Sour Cod*	213.5	171
1 baked potato	8.0	96
4 oz. asparagus, boiled	2.0	20
Salad—endive (1 oz.)	5.1	3
1 T. French Dressing (see Menu 3)	—	88
Coffee Mousse*	31.4	406
	260.0	784
Total for Day	946.7	2064

* Asterisks denote dishes for which recipes are given.
† Decaffeinated coffee may be chosen. It contains 1.7 mg. sodium and 2 calories per cup. With 2 t. milk and 1 t. sugar added, one cup contains 6.5 mg. sodium and 27 calories.

RECIPES FOR MENU 21

Spring Salad

	Milligrams Sodium	Calories
½ oz. lemon gelatin	47.0	60
⅓ cup water	—	—
3 T. diced cucumber	5.5	5
3 T. sliced radishes	25.2	6
1 T. sliced scallions (½ oz.)	1.4	3
½ cup watercress (⅔ oz.)	11.0	2
1 T. mayonnaise	114.2	150
	204.3	226

Dissolve gelatin as directed on package. Add water. Chill until syrupy. Fold in cucumber, radishes and scallions. Serve on watercress with mayonnaise.

Apple Pudding

	Milligrams Sodium	Calories
2 t. butter	.4	76
⅓ cup apple sauce	.1	30
¼ cup brown sugar (1⅓ oz.)	9.1	140
¼ cup dry bread crumbs	143.7	56
4 t. heavy cream	7.6	77
Bit of vanilla extract	—	—
	160.9	379

Melt butter, add apple sauce and sugar. Stir over low heat until browned. Remove. Add vanilla. Chill. Fill sherbet glasses with alternate layers of crumbs and apple sauce mixture. Begin and end with crumbs. Whip cream and place on top.

Sweet and Sour Cod

	Milligrams Sodium	Calories
½ lb. cod (weighed with bones and skin)	184.0	152
½ onion (1 oz.)	1.5	3
½ carrot (1 oz.)	27.0	6
Bit of lemon	—	—
½ t. sugar	—	10
Allspice	1.0	—
	213.5	171

Slice the onion and carrot and place in pot with enough water to cover. Cook about 15 minutes. Then cut in lemon, sugar and a little allspice and place the fish in the pot. Cook for 20 minutes on medium flame after cooking starts.

Coffee Mousse

	Milligrams Sodium	Calories
½ t. unflavored gelatin	—	5
2 t. cold water	—	—
4 t. strong brewed coffee	1.0	—
⅓ cup heavy cream	30.4	306
5 t. powdered sugar	—	95
10 drops vanilla extract	—	—
	31.4	406

Sprinkle gelatin on cold water. Dissolve in hot coffee. Chill until syrupy. Whip cream slightly. Add sugar, vanilla. Fold into coffee mixture. Freeze in tray.

MENU 22

Breakfast	Milligrams Sodium	Calories
2 oz. Kadota figs (2 figs)	.5	100
Puffy Omelet (see Menu 15)	69.0	114
1 sl. whole wheat toast	123.0	70
1 t. butter	.2	38
Coffee†—2 t. cream and 1 t. sugar	3.8	65
	196.5	387

Lunch		
4 oz. orange juice	2.0	44
Salmon Salad*	402.1	275
1 boiled potato	4.0	92
2 Tea Cookies (see Menu 2)	7.4	154
Coffee†—2 t. cream and 1 t. sugar	3.8	65
	419.3	630

Dinner		
Pan-Broiled Pork Chops with Apple*	73.0	377
Baked sweet potato	20.4	92
Spinach*	117.0	137
Hearts of lettuce (2 oz.)	6.8	6
Baked Custard*	105.6	203
Coffee†—2 t. cream and 1 t. sugar	3.8	65
2 Tea Cookies (see Menu 13)	7.4	154
	334.0	1034
Total for Day	949.8	2051

* Asterisks denote dishes for which recipes are given.
† Decaffeinated coffee may be chosen. It contains 1.7 mg. sodium and 2 calories per cup. With 2 t. milk and 1 t. sugar added, one cup contains 6.5 mg. sodium and 27 calories.

RECIPES FOR MENU 22

Salmon Salad

	Milligrams Sodium	Calories
2 oz. canned salmon (about 5 T.)	268.4	120
1 T. diced celery (½ oz.)	19.5	1
2 t. minced green pepper	—	4
1 T. mayonnaise	114.2	150
	402.1	275

Bone the salmon and flake. Combine with celery, green pepper and mayonnaise. Serve on lettuce.

Pan-Broiled Pork Chops with Apple

½ lb. pork chops, lean (weighed with bone)	70.4	304
Pepper	—	—
1 T. flour	.2	33
1 apple	2.4	40
	73.0	377

Wipe chops and sprinkle with pepper; dust lightly with flour. Place in hot heavy frying pan, fat edge down. Brown on both sides. Pour off fat, cover and cook slowly until tender (about 25 minutes). Core and pare apple. Cut in ½" slices. Fry in fat remaining in pan and serve with chops.

Spinach

1 t. minced onion	—	—
1 T. butter	.7	113
½ cup hot chopped spinach (3⅓ oz.)	116.3	24
Pepper	—	—
	117.0	137

Saute onion in butter, pour over spinach and add pepper. Mix thoroughly.

Baked Custard

	Milligrams Sodium	Calories
1 egg	67.0	77
1⅓ T. sugar	—	75
⅓ cup milk	38.6	51
⅙ t. vanilla	—	—
Nutmeg	—	—
	105.6	203

Beat egg slightly. Add sugar; mix well. Scald milk. Add slowly, stirring constantly. Add vanilla extract. Pour into baking dish. Sprinkle with nutmeg. Set in pan of cold water. Bake in moderate oven 1¼ hours.

MENU 23

Breakfast	Milligrams Sodium	Calories
½ grapefruit	.8	12
1 Old-Fashioned Pancake*	253.5	629
1 t. unsalted butter	.2	38
Hot Blueberry Sauce*	.8	67
1 glass low-fat milk	127.4	125
	382.7	871

Lunch		
Garden Salad (see Menu 12)	23.1	17
2 T. Tarragon Vinegar (see Menu 12)	6.2	1
1 cup Minestrone Soup* with	40.6	172
1 T. Parmesan cheese, grated	38.0	20
1 sl. Parmesan Toast*	41.7	155
¾ cup steamed zucchini with sprinkle of nutmeg	.5	20
1 glass low-fat milk	127.4	125
	277.5	510

Dinner		
6 oz. Veal Scallopini with Marsala*	193.6	335
¼ cup long grain brown rice	2.8	167
Very Green Salad*	20.0	142
1 T. Tarragon Vinegar and Oil Dressing*	1.5	89
½ cup steamed carrots	52.3	13
1 t. unsalted butter	.2	38
Decaffeinated coffee (no cream or sugar)	1.7	2
	272.1	786
Total for Day	932.3	2167

* Asterisks denote dishes for which recipes are given.

RECIPES FOR MENU 23

Old-Fashioned Pancakes

	Milligrams Sodium	Calories
½ cup all-purpose flour	1.4	240
1 egg	67.0	77
2 egg whites	110.0	37
1½ T. vegetable oil	—	184
½ cup low-fat milk	75.0	72
1 t. white sugar (optional)	.2	19
¼ t. vanilla extract	—	—
	253.6	629

Combine the egg, milk and sugar. Then add the flour, stirring until smooth. Beat the egg whites until they become very stiff. Fold the whites into the batter. Grease skillet with a few drops of oil and cook over moderate heat.

Hot Blueberry Sauce

1 t. unsalted butter	.2	38
¼ cup blueberries	.2	19
½ t. honey	.4	10
	.8	67

Heat butter in skillet. Add blueberries and saute briefly. Add honey. Pour over pancakes.

Minestrone Soup

Makes about 6 cups.

	Milligrams Sodium	Calories
6 cups water	—	—
¼ cup dried kidney beans	18.4	125
¼ cup lentils	6.8	58
2 T. olive oil	—	264
1 cup diced white onion	16.0	37
1½ cups cubed carrots	156.8	38
¼ cup fresh peas	.4	27
1 cup chopped tomatoes	5.4	25
1 cup diced zucchini	1.3	29
¼ cup fresh parsley, finely chopped	5.0	3
2 cloves garlic, pressed	3.4	8
4 oz. small elbow macaroni	29.4	418
¼ t. rosemary	.1	—
½ T. dried basil	.6	—
Pepper to taste	—	—
	243.6	1032

One 1-cup serving equals 40.6 mg. sodium and 172 calories

Soak kidney beans and lentils overnight. Cook until tender. Saute the onion, carrots, zucchini and pressed garlic cloves for about 10 minutes. Remove from heat and add the peas and tomatoes. Add the mixed vegetables and herbs to the beans and water. Bring to a boil and simmer for 20 minutes. Add the elbow macaroni and cook for 15 minutes longer or until macaroni is tender. Add pepper to taste.

Parmesan Toast

1 sl. Low-Sodium Bread (see Menu 1)	3.5	97
1 t. unsalted butter	.2	38
1 T. Parmesan cheese, grated	38.0	20
	41.7	155

Butter bread. Sprinkle with Parmesan and toast in toaster oven or bake in 400° oven.

Veal Scallopini with Marsala

Makes 2 servings.

	Milligrams Sodium	Calories
¾ lb. veal cutlet	374.6	371
2½ T. flour	.4	75
1 t. unsalted butter	.5	35
2 t. olive oil	—	88
1 cup sliced mushrooms	6.3	9
1 clove garlic	1.7	4
¼ cup fresh tomatoes, diced	1.4	6
¼ cup dry marsala	2.0	82
½ t. dried basil	.2	—
1 t. chopped parsley	—	—
Sprinkle pepper	—	—
	387.1	670

One 6-oz. serving equals 193.6 mg. sodium and 335 calories

Preheat oven to 325°. Flour the veal cutlet. Sprinkle with pepper. Brown on both sides in the butter and oil combined. Add the rest of the vegetables and the wine. Put in a casserole. Cover and bake for 40 minutes.

Very Green Salad

1½ cups Romaine lettuce, torn in bite-size pieces (about 5 large lettuce leaves)	7.4	10
1 T. Bermuda onion, chopped	1.0	2
½ cup thinly sliced cucumber	9.1	7
½ cup chopped green pepper	1.5	11
¼ avocado cut into ½" pieces	1.0	112
	20.0	142

Mix cut and chopped vegetables together.

Tarragon Vinegar and Oil Dressing

Makes about 6 tablespoons.

	Milligrams Sodium	Calories
¼ cup olive oil	—	528
2 T. white or red wine vinegar	6.0	1
1 t. dried tarragon	1.0	—
⅛ t. pepper	—	—
1 small garlic clove, crushed	1.7	4
	8.1	533

1 T. serving equals 1.5 mg. sodium and 89 calories

Add the tarragon and pepper and crushed garlic clove to the wine vinegar. Shake well. Pour the olive oil into the mixture and shake again.

MENU 24

Breakfast	Milligrams Sodium	Calories
Blackberry Yogurt Shake*	176.3	159
2 sls. whole wheat toast	246.0	140
2 t. unsalted butter	.4	76
1 cup hot apple cider with cinnamon stick or sprinkles cinnamon	2.0	117
	424.7	492

Lunch		
Fresh Tomato Pasta*	94.9	837
3 T. Parmesan cheese, grated	114.0	60
1 cup steamed broccoli	10.6	20
2 T. lemon juice	.6	2
1 Hot Roll (see Menu 5)	8.0	77
1 t. unsalted butter	.2	38
Herb tea (without caffeine)	—	—
	228.3	1034

Dinner		
Baked Lemon Sole in Wine*	144.0	439
4 oz. Tabbouleh Salad*	6.9	194
½ cup steamed spinach with sprinkle tarragon and few squeezes lemon juice	90.0	22
¼ cup steamed carrots sprinkled with marjoram	26.1	6
Decaffeinated coffee (no cream or sugar)	1.7	2
	268.7	663
Total for Day	921.7	2189

* Asterisks denote dishes for which recipes are given.

RECIPES FOR MENU 24

Blackberry Yogurt Shake

	Milligrams Sodium	Calories
8 oz. plain low-fat yogurt	172.5	118
1 t. honey (if desired)	.9	20
½ cup fresh or frozen unsweetened blackberries	2.9	21
	176.3	159

Mix yogurt, honey and blackberries in blender. Pour into glass.

Fresh Tomato Pasta

Makes about 2 cups.

	Milligrams Sodium	Calories
4 oz. dry pasta (2 cups)	29.5	420
3 cups unpeeled ripe tomatoes (about 2 lbs.)	16.2	76
3 T. unsalted tomato paste (optional)	32.3	41
2 cloves garlic, minced	3.4	8
¾ cup onion, chopped	12.0	28
1 t. oregano	3	—
1 T. dried basil	1.2	—
Pepper to taste	—	—
	94.9	573

Liquefy raw tomatoes first in a blender or food processor if one is available. If not, mash tomatoes well, and again when they are cooking later on. Saute the chopped onion in the olive oil over low flame until yellow. Add the tomatoes, garlic, basil, oregano and pepper. If using the tomato paste, add now. Stir and bring to a boil. Simmer for about 30 minutes until the sauce thickens. Serve over hot pasta.

Baked Lemon Sole in Wine

	Milligrams Sodium	Calories
4 oz. piece lemon sole	107.9	92
2 T. olive oil	—	264
½ cup chopped onion	8.0	18
½ cup sliced tomato	2.7	13
¼ cup white wine	12.2	44
Freshly ground pepper	—	—
1 t. Parmesan cheese	13.0	7
2 t. fresh lemon juice	.2	1
	144.0	439

Preheat oven to 400°. Sprinkle olive oil and Parmesan over the fish. Place sliced tomato on top. Put the chopped onion around the fish. Cook for 5 minutes. Pour wine into dish and baste. Cook for another 5 minutes, basting again. Use lemon juice as desired.

Tabbouleh Salad

Makes 7 servings.

4 cups boiling water	—	—
1¼ cups bulgur wheat	—	743
½ cup chopped scallions	4.0	29
1½ cups fresh minced parsley	29.7	19
2 cups tomatoes, chopped	10.8	50
½ cup fresh minced mint	—	—
¾ cup fresh lemon juice	3.7	13
¼ cup olive oil	.1	503
Pepper	—	—
	48.3	1357

One 4-oz. serving equals 6.9 mg. sodium and 194 calories

Pour water on bulgur wheat. Let stand for 2 hours, until the wheat is fluffy. Strain excess water. Combine parsley, mint, the tomatoes, scallions, lemon juice and olive oil. Mix with the wheat. Add pepper to taste. Chill 1½ hours. Serve on raw lettuce or cabbage leaves.

MENUS 25–36

Weight-Reducing Meals
400–500 Milligrams of Sodium
Less Than 1200 Calories

A portion of the weight of the obese person consists of water bound to sodium in his tissues. This excess water may be liberated and excreted during the maintenance of the low-sodium diet. In addition, the low-sodium diet tends to decrease the hydrochloric acid production in the stomach thereby decreasing hunger. The low-sodium diets for reducing which follow will be found to be of help in the program of weight reduction.

MENU 25

Breakfast	Milligrams Sodium	Calories
4 oz. orange juice (½ cup)	2.0	44
¼ cup oatmeal (1 oz.)	9.5	115
½ cup milk	58.0	76
Coffee† (no sugar or cream)	—	8
1 sl. Low-Sodium Bread (see Menu 1)	3.5	97
	73.0	340

Lunch		
Scrambled Egg and Mushrooms (see Menu 1)	81.1	130
Salad—½ grapefruit, 1 oz. lettuce	4.2	15
Cherry and Banana Gelatin*	47.6	137
Coffee† (no sugar or cream)	—	8
	132.9	290

Dinner		
½ lb. broiled liver	195.2	328
4 oz. mashed yellow turnips	5.6	56
Eggplant Mexican*	23.2	40
Salad—2 oz. lettuce and 1 medium tomato	10.0	22
4 t. Vinegar Dressing*	3.0	19
Baked apple with	2.4	40
1 t. sugar and cinnamon	—	19
Coffee†—2 t. milk and 1 t. sugar	4.8	33
	244.2	557
Total for Day	450.1	1173

* Asterisks denote dishes for which recipes are given.
† Decaffeinated coffee may be chosen. It contains 1.7 mg. sodium and 2 calories per cup. With 2 t. milk and 1 t. sugar added, one cup contains 6.5 mg. sodium and 27 calories.

RECIPES FOR MENU 25

Cherry and Banana Gelatin

Makes 2 servings.

	Milligrams Sodium	Calories
1 pkge. cherry gelatin (1 oz.)	94.2	120
⅔ cup water	—	—
⅓ cup sliced bananas (2 oz.)	.6	44
⅓ cup pitted canned black cherries (2½ oz.)	.5	110
	95.3	274

One portion equals 47.6 mg. sodium and 137 calories.

Dissolve gelatin in water as directed. Chill until syrupy. Beat until frothy. Fold in fruit and chill.

Eggplant Mexican

4 oz. eggplant	2.8	16
½ cup tomatoes (4 oz.)	20.4	24
½ t. minced onion	—	—
⅙ t. chili powder	—	—
Pepper and bit of garlic	—	—
	23.2	40

Pare and cut eggplant into cubes. Add remaining ingredients. Simmer 1 hour or until eggplant is tender.

Vinegar Dressing

1 T. vinegar	3.0	0
1 t. sugar	—	19
	3.0	19

Combine ingredients.

MENU 26

Breakfast	Milligrams Sodium	Calories
1 orange, sliced	2.4	32
1 T. rice (cooked) with	1.2	68
½ cup hot milk	58.0	76
1 sl. Low-Sodium Bread (see Menu 1)	3.5	97
1 t. butter (unsalted)	.2	38
Coffee* (without cream or sugar)	—	8
	65.3	319

Lunch		
1 Fried Egg and Mashed Potatoes (see Menu 2)	72.8	249
1 cup fruit salad, canned (4 oz.)	10.0	80
Coffee* (without cream or sugar)	—	8
	82.8	337

Dinner		
½ lb. broiled shoulder lamb chops, lean only (weighed with fat and bone)	136.0	288
4 oz. boiled peas	—	56
1 boiled parsley potato	4.0	92
3 oz. celery hearts (about 2)	116.7	9
4 t. Vinegar Dressing (see Menu 25)	3.0	19
Canned pears, 2 halves (4 oz.)	9.2	72
Coffee*—2 t. milk and 1 t. sugar	4.8	33
	273.7	569
Total for Day	421.8	1225

* Decaffeinated coffee may be chosen. It contains 1.7 mg. sodium and 2 calories per cup. With 2 t. milk and 1 t. sugar added, one cup contains 6.5 mg. sodium and 27 calories.

MENU 27

Breakfast	Milligrams Sodium	Calories
½ grapefruit, sliced (4 oz.)	.8	12
1 Shredded Wheat biscuit (1 oz.) with	4.7	103
½ banana (2½ oz.) with	.7	55
½ cup milk	58.0	76
1 sl. Low-Sodium Bread (see Menu 1)	3.5	97
Coffee* (without cream or sugar)	—	8
	67.7	351

Lunch		
Spanish Omelet (see Menu 3)	93.0	136
1 sl. Low-Sodium Bread (see Menu 1)	3.5	97
1 cup canned pineapple (5 oz.)	1.4	90
Coffee* (without cream or sugar)	—	8
	97.9	331

Dinner		
Sweet and Sour Cod (see Menu 21)	213.5	171
Baked potato	8.2	96
Diced Carrots with Minted Peas (see Menu 3)	28.9	65
Hearts of lettuce (2 oz.)	6.8	6
4 t. Vinegar Dressing (see Menu 25)	3.0	19
Pineapple and Cocoanut (see Menu 3)	3.4	123
	263.8	480
Total for Day	429.4	1162

* Decaffeinated coffee may be chosen. It contains 1.7 mg. sodium and 2 calories per cup. With 2 t. milk and 1 t. sugar added, one cup contains 6.5 mg. sodium and 27 calories.

MENU 28

Breakfast	Milligrams Sodium	Calories
8 oz. orange juice	4.0	88
1 cup Puffed Rice (½ oz.)	.1	60
½ cup milk	58.0	76
Coffee*—2 t. milk and 1 t. sugar	4.8	33
	66.9	257

Lunch		
Mushroom Omelet (see Menu 4)	73.8	127
2 oz. lettuce and ½ tomato	8.0	14
1 sl. Low-Sodium Bread (see Menu 1)	3.5	97
1 t. butter	.2	38
Coffee* (without cream or sugar)	—	8
	85.5	284

Dinner		
½ grapefruit with 1 t. honey	2.3	39
Meat Loaf (see Menu 15)	255.1	297
1 boiled parsley potato	4.0	92
Endive salad (¼ small head)	2.6	1
4 t. Vinegar Dressing (see Menu 25)	3.0	19
Apple Sauce Supreme (see Menu 4)	30.7	86
Coffee*—2 t. milk and 1 t. sugar	4.8	33
	302.5	567
Total for Day	454.9	1108

* Decaffeinated coffee may be chosen. It contains 1.7 mg. sodium and 2 calories per cup. With 2 t. milk and 1 t. sugar added, one cup contains 6.5 mg. sodium and 27 calories.

MENU 29

Breakfast	Milligrams Sodium	Calories
4 oz. strawberries, with	1.6	28
1 t. sugar	—	19
1 cup Puffed Wheat (¹/₂ oz.)	.4	55
¹/₂ banana, cut into cereal (2 oz.)	.6	44
¹/₂ cup milk	58.0	76
Coffee* (without cream or sugar)	—	8
	60.6	230

Lunch		
Asparagus Omelet (Menu 18)	68.1	87
1 Hot Roll (Menu 5)	8.0	77
Salad—¹/₂ orange, 2 oz. lettuce	8.0	22
Coffee*—2 t. milk and 1 t. sugar	4.8	33
	88.9	219

Dinner		
8 oz. Breaded Veal Cutlet (see Menu 5)	240.8	488
1 baked potato	8.0	96
4 oz. Brussels Sprouts (see Menu 5)	9.1	69
Salad—1 oz. cucumber, 1 oz. lettuce, ¹/₂ tomato, 1 oz. green pepper	8.8	22
4 oz. fruit salad (canned)	10.0	80
Coffee* (without cream or sugar)	—	8
	276.7	763
Total for Day	426.2	1212

* Decaffeinated coffee may be chosen. It contains 1.7 mg. sodium and 2 calories per cup. With 2 t. milk and 1 t. sugar added, one cup contains 6.5 mg. sodium and 27 calories.

MENU 30

Breakfast	Milligrams Sodium	Calories
4 oz. apricot nectar (½ cup)	2.0	68
¼ cup Instant Ralston (1 oz.) with	.2	110
½ cup milk	58.0	76
Coffee*—2 t. milk and 1 t. sugar	4.8	33
	65.0	287

Lunch		
Spicy Creamed Egg (see Menu 4)	106.5	225
1 boiled mashed potato	4.0	92
Salad—½ apple, ½ grapefruit (sliced) on 1 leaf lettuce	5.4	35
Coffee* (without cream or sugar)	—	8
	115.9	360

Dinner		
Braised Veal Chop (see Menu 19)	244.9	315
Baked potato	8.0	96
1 t. butter	.2	38
2 oz. hearts of lettuce	6.8	6
4 t. Vinegar Dressing (see Menu 25)	3.0	19
½ cup apple sauce (4½ oz.)	.4	45
Coffee*—2 t. milk and 1 t. sugar	4.8	33
	268.1	552
Total for Day	449.0	1199

* Decaffeinated coffee may be chosen. It contains 1.7 mg. sodium and 2 calories per cup. With 2 t. milk and 1 t. sugar added, one cup contains 6.5 mg. sodium and 27 calories.

MENU 31

Breakfast	Milligrams Sodium	Calories
1 orange, sliced	2.4	32
1 cup Puffed Rice (½ oz.) with	.1	60
2 oz. blueberries with	.2	30
½ cup milk	58.0	76
1 sl. Low-Sodium Bread (see Menu 1)	3.5	97
Coffee* (without cream or sugar)	—	8
	64.2	303

Lunch		
Spring Salad (see Menu 21)	204.3	226
1 sl. Low-Sodium Bread (see Menu 1)	3.5	97
¼ cantaloupe (3⅓ oz.)	12.6	23
Coffee*—2 t. milk and 1 t. sugar	4.8	33
	225.2	379

Dinner		
½ lb. Pan-Browned Pork Chops (see Menu 7)	70.6	304
with Creole Sauce (make 2 portions, one		
for next day's lunch for spaghetti)	5.0	20
1 baked sweet potato	20.4	92
2½ oz. Candied Carrots (see Menu 7)	68.1	62
½ oz. endive salad (¼ head) with	2.6	1
4 t. Vinegar Dressing (see Menu 25)	3.0	19
Coffee* (without cream or sugar)	—	8
	169.7	506
Total for Day	459.1	1188

* Decaffeinated coffee may be chosen. It contains 1.7 mg. sodium and 2 calories per cup. With 2 t. milk and 1 t. sugar added, one cup contains 6.5 mg. sodium and 27 calories.

MENU 32

Breakfast	Milligrams Sodium	Calories
4 oz. grapefruit juice, unsweetened	.4	40
2 t. farina (²⁄₃ oz.) (Do not use the quick cooking type) with	.1	67
½ cup milk	58.0	76
Coffee* (without cream or sugar)	—	8
	58.5	191

Lunch		
1 scrambled egg (use 1 t. butter for frying)	67.2	115
2 oz. spaghetti with	4.4	64
Creole Sauce (see Menu 7)	5.0	20
Salad—½ tomato and 1 oz. lettuce	5.0	11
Coffee* (without cream or sugar)	—	8
	81.6	218

Dinner		
Baked Chicken (see Menu 16)	216.7	509
1 mashed potato	4.0	92
4 oz. boiled cabbage	25.6	28
Salad—2 oz. lettuce and ½ sliced orange	8.0	22
Cherry and Banana Gelatin (see Menu 25)	47.6	137
Coffee* (without cream or sugar)	—	8
	301.9	796
Total for Day	442.0	1205

* Decaffeinated coffee may be chosen. It contains 1.7 mg. sodium and 2 calories per cup. With 2 t. milk and 1 t. sugar added, one cup contains 6.5 mg. sodium and 27 calories.

MENU 33

Breakfast	Milligrams Sodium	Calories
½ grapefruit	.8	12
¼ cup Maltex Cereal	1.1	110
½ cup milk	58.0	76
Coffee* (without cream or sugar)	—	8
	59.9	206

Lunch		
Strained Vegetable Soup (see Menu 9)	62.3	133
French Omelet (see Menu 9)	67.2	115
Salad—1 oz. cucumber, 1 oz. lettuce, ½ tomato	8.7	14
4 t. Vinegar Dressing (see Menu 25)	3.0	19
1 Hot Roll (see Menu 5)	8.0	77
Coffee* (without cream or sugar)	—	8
	149.2	366

Dinner		
Baked Cod in Milk (see Menu 9)	229.7	394
1 boiled potato	4.0	92
Eggplant Mexican (see Menu 25)	23.2	40
Salad—½ sliced apple, ½ sliced banana, shredded lettuce leaf	5.1	56
Coffee* (without cream or sugar)	—	8
	262.0	590
Total for Day	471.1	1162

* Decaffeinated coffee may be chosen. It contains 1.7 mg. sodium and 2 calories per cup. With 2 t. milk and 1 t. sugar added, one cup contains 6.5 mg. sodium and 27 calories.

MENU 34

Breakfast	Milligrams Sodium	Calories
4 oz. canned pears (2 halves)	9.2	72
1 boiled egg	67.0	77
1 Hot Roll (see Menu 5)	8.0	77
1 t. butter	.2	38
Coffee†—2 t. milk and 1 t. sugar	4.8	33
	89.2	297

Lunch		
Cucumbers in Sour Cream (see Menu 10)	15.6	119
1 Hot Roll (see Menu 5)	8.0	77
Cantaloupe Gelatin Salad (see Menu 19)	17.4	73
Coffee†—2 t. milk and 1 t. sugar	4.8	33
	45.8	302

Dinner		
Liver Saute*	125.0	270
1 baked potato and 1 t. butter	8.2	134
¼ lb. string beans and 1 t. butter	3.8	46
Stuffed Celery (see Menu 17)	112.7	25
2½ oz. ice cream	71.2	145
	320.9	620
Total for Day	455.9	1219

* Asterisk denotes dish for which recipe is given.
† Decaffeinated coffee may be chosen. It contains 1.7 mg. sodium and 2 calories per cup. With 2 t. milk and 1 t. sugar added, one cup contains 6.5 mg. sodium and 27 calories.

RECIPE FOR MENU 34

Liver Saute

	Milligrams Sodium	Calories
4 oz. calf's liver, dredged in flour	124.0	228
Flour	—	20
$^1/_6$ onion, chopped	.9	—
1 peppercorn and pepper	—	3
$^1/_2$ t. butter	.1	19
Bit of bay leaf and shredded lemon peel	—	—
	125.0	270

Wash liver in cold water. Rub with pepper. Dredge with flour and brown quickly in browned butter. Add onion, bay leaf, lemon peel, 2 T. water and peppercorn. Cover pot and cook slowly 20 minutes or until tender. Remove to hot platter and strain gravy over the meat. Garnish with chopped parsley.

MENU 35

Breakfast	Milligrams Sodium	Calories
1 Shredded Wheat Biscuit (1 oz.) with	4.7	103
¼ cup strawberries	.8	10
½ cup low-fat milk	63.7	63
1 sl. Low-Sodium Bread (see Menu 1), toasted with a sprinkle of cinnamon	3.5	97
1 t. apple butter	—	11
Herb tea (without caffeine)	—	—
	72.7	284

Lunch		
Sweet and Sour Chicken Salad*	125.2	216
8 t. Sweet and Sour Sauce*	5.7	70
½ cup steamed cauliflower dipped in Tangy Yogurt Dressing*	17.0	16
¼ cup raw long grain brown rice, boiled	2.8	167
Sprinkle turmeric for rice	—	—
Decaffeinated coffee or	1.7	2
Herb tea (without caffeine)	—	—
	152.4	471

Dinner		
¼ lb. Dill Baked Salmon*	132.6	232
Garden Salad (see Menu 12)	23.1	17
2 T. Tarragon Vinegar (see Menu 12)	6.2	1
½ cup steamed broccoli	5.3	10
1 T. lemon juice for broccoli	.3	1
1 Hot Roll (see Menu 5)	8.0	77
1 t. unsalted butter	.2	38
Herb tea (without caffeine)	—	—
	175.7	376
Total for Day	400.8	1131

* Asterisks denote dishes for which recipes are given.

RECIPES FOR MENU 35

Sweet and Sour Chicken Salad

	Milligrams Sodium	Calories
1½ cups Romaine lettuce, torn	7.4	10
¼ cup cooked chicken breast meat (skin removed)	28.7	99
¼ cup thinly sliced mushrooms	1.6	2
¼ cup scallions, chopped	2.5	6
1½ long stalks of celery, finely chopped	84.0	3
2 T. slivered almonds	1.0	96
	125.2	216

Mix all the ingredients together. Add Sweet and Sour Sauce (see next recipe).

Sweet and Sour Sauce

Makes ⅓ cup.
(Enough for 2 servings of 8 t. each.)

	Milligrams Sodium	Calories
2 T. honey	4.6	120
¼ cup orange juice	2.5	20
4 t. cider vinegar	4.0	—
¾ t. dry mustard	—	—
¾ t. turmeric	.2	—
¼ t. ginger	—	—
	11.3	140

One serving of 8 t. equals 5.7 mg. sodium and 70 calories

Place the honey and orange juice in a saucepan and simmer until the liquid is slightly reduced. Then add the cider vinegar, mustard, turmeric and ginger to the simmering pan. Chill. Use over chicken salad.

Tangy Yogurt Dressing

	Milligrams Sodium	Calories
2 T. plain low-fat yogurt	15.9	16
1 t. fresh lemon juice	.1	—
⅛ t. dried parsley	.7	—
¼ t. dried tarragon	.3	—
Pepper to taste	—	—
	17.0	16

Combine the ingredients and serve chilled with cooked cauliflower.

Dill Baked Salmon

Makes 2 servings.

	Milligrams Sodium	Calories
½ lb. salmon fillet or steak	249.5	447
1 T. plain low-fat yogurt	11.6	8
¼ cup onion, chopped	4.0	9
¼ t. dill	—	—
	265.1	464

One ¼-lb. serving equals 132.6 mg. sodium and 232 calories.

Put salmon in a greased oven dish and spread yogurt over it. Sprinkle the chopped onion and dill on top. Cover and bake at 350° for about 20 minutes. If you use foil to bake it, be sure to seal the fold and allow approximately the same amount of time.

MENU 36

Breakfast	Milligrams Sodium	Calories
1 cup apple juice	117.0	2
1 cup Puffed Rice (½ oz.) with	.1	60
½ banana (about 2½ oz.) with	.7	55
½ cup low-fat milk	63.7	63
Herb tea or	—	—
Decaffeinated coffee (without cream or sugar)	1.7	2
	183.2	182

Lunch		
10 oz. Black Bean Soup with Wine*	46.9	277
Very Green Salad (see Menu 23)	20.0	142
2 T. Tarragon Vinegar (see Menu 12)	6.2	1
Herb tea (without caffeine) or	—	—
Decaffeinated coffee (without cream or sugar)	1.7	2
	74.8	422

Dinner		
6 oz. Easy Herb Chicken*	138.2	272
Tomato Eggplant Italienne*	39.7	105
¼ cup long grain brown rice, cooked	2.8	167
2 oz. hearts of lettuce	6.8	6
4 t. Vinegar Dressing (see Menu 21)	3.0	19
Herb tea (without caffeine) or	—	—
Decaffeinated coffee (no cream or sugar)	1.7	2
	192.2	571
Total for Day	450.2	1175

* Asterisks denote dishes for which recipes are given.

RECIPES FOR MENU 36
Black Bean Soup with Wine

Makes 2 servings.

	Milligrams Sodium	Calories
2 cups water	—	—
½ cup black beans	25.0	339
½ cup diced onion	8.0	18
½ cup diced carrots	52.2	12
½ cup chopped tomatoes	2.7	13
1 T. olive oil	—	132
1 clove garlic, minced	1.7	4
2 T. dry sherry	3.0	35
1 T. chopped parsley	1.2	1
Dash of cumin	—	—
⅛ t. oregano	—	—
Dash pepper, freshly ground	—	—
	93.8	554

One 10-oz. serving equals 46.9 mg. sodium and 277 calories

Soak beans overnight. Cook the beans in water with a clove of garlic for 2 to 2½ hours. Saute onion, garlic and the vegetables in the oil for about 3 minutes, sprinkling with pepper. Add this vegetable mixture to the beans. Add 1 more cup of water to the saucepan and heat through, stirring frequently. At serving time, pour 1 T. sherry into the soup bowl and place some fresh parsley on top.

Easy Herb Chicken

Makes 2 servings.

	Milligrams Sodium	Calories
¾ lb. breast meat only (not weighed with rest of chicken)	275.4	412
Garlic	—	—
1 T. olive oil	—	132
¼ t. marjoram	.3	—
¼ t. thyme	.3	—
1 t. chopped parsley	.4	—
1 T. unsalted butter	.9	114
	277.3	658

One 6-oz. serving equals 138.6 mg. sodium and 329 calories

Wash and rub chicken with garlic. Put in greased baking dish. Sprinkle the pieces with thyme and marjoram and place covered in the refrigerator. Remove, sprinkle with parsley and pepper and dot with unsalted butter. Bake for 35 to 45 minutes in a 400° oven.

Tomato Eggplant Italienne

	Milligrams Sodium	Calories
¾ cup peeled and sliced eggplant	1.5	9
1 t. olive oil	—	44
1 garlic clove	1.7	4
¼ cup chopped onions	4.0	9
3 T. unsalted tomato paste	32.3	41
½ cup water	—	—
½ t. dried basil	.2	—
¼ t. dried oregano	—	—
	39.7	107

Saute the onion in the olive oil. Add the garlic and saute briefly. Add the tomato paste and water and bring to a boil for a moment. Lower heat, add herbs and simmer until sauce thickens. Meanwhile, steam the eggplant. Pour sauce, when ready, over the eggplant and serve.

MENUS 37–48

Weight-Reducing Menus
Less Than 350 Milligrams of Sodium
Less Than 1200 Calories

MENU 37

Breakfast	Milligrams Sodium	Calories
4 oz. orange juice (½ cup)	2.0	44
¼ cup oatmeal (1 oz.)	9.5	115
½ cup milk	58.0	76
1 sl. Low-Sodium Bread (see Menu 1)	3.5	97
Coffee* (without cream or sugar)	—	8
	73.0	340

Lunch		
Scrambled Eggs and Mushrooms (see Menu 1)	81.1	130
Salad—½ grapefruit, 1 oz. lettuce	4.2	15
3 canned prunes (3⅓ oz.)	2.8	100
Coffee* (without cream or sugar)	—	8
	88.1	253

Dinner		
6 oz. broiled liver	146.4	246
4 oz. fresh boiled peas	—	56
4 oz. mashed yellow turnips	5.6	56
Salad—2 oz. lettuce and 1 medium tomato	10.0	22
4 t. Vinegar Dressing (see Menu 25)	3.0	19
Baked apple with	2.4	40
1 t. sugar and cinnamon	—	19
Coffee*—2 t. milk and 1 t. sugar	4.8	33
	172.2	491
Total for Day	333.3	1084

* Decaffeinated coffee may be chosen. It contains 1.7 mg. sodium and 2 calories per cup. With 2 t. milk and 1 t. sugar added, one cup contains 6.5 mg. sodium and 27 calories.

MENU 38

Breakfast	Milligrams Sodium	Calories
1 orange, sliced	2.4	32
1 T. rice, cooked, with	1.2	68
½ cup milk	58.0	76
1 sl. Low-Sodium Bread (see Menu 1)	3.5	97
1 t. butter (unsalted)	.2	38
Coffee* (without cream or sugar)	—	8
	65.3	319

Lunch		
1 Fried Egg and Mashed Potatoes (see Menu 2)	72.8	249
1 cup fruit salad, canned (4 oz.)	10.0	80
Coffee* (without cream or sugar)	—	8
	82.8	337

Dinner		
½ lb. broiled shoulder lamb chops, lean only (weighed with fat and bone)	136.0	288
4 oz. boiled peas	—	56
1 boiled parsley potato	4.0	92
Salad—1 oz. cucumber, ½ tomato and 1 oz. lettuce	8.7	14
4 t. Vinegar Dressing (see Menu 25)	3.0	19
2 halves canned pears (4 oz.)	9.2	72
	160.9	541
Total for Day	309.0	1197

* Decaffeinated coffee may be chosen. It contains 1.7 mg. sodium and 2 calories per cup. With 2 t. milk and 1 t. sugar added, one cup contains 6.5 mg. sodium and 27 calories.

MENU 39

Breakfast	Milligrams Sodium	Calories
½ grapefruit, sliced (4 oz.)	.8	12
1 Shredded Wheat biscuit (1 oz.) with	4.7	103
½ banana (2½ oz.) with	.7	55
½ cup milk	58.0	76
1 sl. Low-Sodium Bread (see Menu 1)	3.5	97
Coffee* (without cream or sugar)	—	8
	67.7	351

Lunch		
Spanish Omelet (see Menu 3)	93.0	136
1 sl. Low-Sodium Bread (see Menu 1)	3.5	97
1 cup canned pineapple (5 oz.)	1.4	90
Coffee*—2 t. milk and 1 t. sugar	4.8	33
	102.7	356

Dinner		
Broiled Flounder (see Menu 17)	146.0	159
Baked potato	8.2	96
Diced Carrots with Minted Peas (see Menu 3)	28.9	65
Hearts of lettuce (2 oz.)	6.8	6
4 t. Vinegar Dressing (see Menu 25)	3.0	19
Pineapple and Cocoanut (see Menu 3)	3.4	123
	196.3	468
Total for Day	366.7	1175

* Decaffeinated coffee may be chosen. It contains 1.7 mg. sodium and 2 calories per cup. With 2 t. milk and 1 t. sugar added, one cup contains 6.5 mg. sodium and 27 calories.

MENU 40

Breakfast	Milligrams Sodium	Calories
8 oz. orange juice	4.0	88
1 cup Puffed Rice (½ oz.)	.1	60
½ cup milk	58.0	76
Coffee*—2 t. milk and 1 t. sugar	4.8	33
	66.9	257

Lunch		
Mushroom Omelet (see Menu 4)	73.8	127
2 oz. lettuce and ½ tomato	8.4	14
1 sl. Low-Sodium Bread (see Menu 1)	3.5	97
1 t. butter	.2	38
Coffee* (without cream or sugar)	—	8
	85.9	284

Dinner		
½ grapefruit with 1 t. honey	2.3	39
Beef Stew (⅔ recipe for today, ⅓ for tomorrow's lunch) (see Menu 4)	151.4	386
1 sl. Low-Sodium Bread (see Menu 1)	3.5	97
Endive salad (¼ small head)	2.6	1
4 t. Vinegar Dressing (see Menu 25)	3.0	19
4 T. canned pineapple (1¼ oz.)	.3	22
Coffee* (without cream or sugar)	—	8
	163.1	572
Total for Day	315.9	1113

* Decaffeinated coffee may be chosen. It contains 1.7 mg. sodium and 2 calories per cup. With 2 t. milk and 1 t. sugar added, one cup contains 6.5 mg. sodium and 27 calories.

MENU 41

Breakfast	Milligrams Sodium	Calories
4 oz. strawberries with	1.6	28
1 t. sugar	—	17
1 cup Puffed Wheat (½ oz.)	.4	55
½ banana cut into cereal (2 oz.)	.6	44
½ cup milk	58.0	76
Coffee* (without cream or sugar)	—	8
	60.6	228

Lunch		
Beef Stew, left from yesterday's meal (see Menu 5)	76.0	193
1 Hot Roll (see Menu 5)	8.0	77
Salad—½ orange, 2 oz. lettuce	8.0	22
Coffee*—2 t. milk and 1 t. sugar	4.8	33
	96.8	325

Dinner		
Macaroni with Liver (see Menu 14)	79.6	231
4 oz. string beans, boiled, with	3.6	8
1 t. butter	—	38
3 oz. yellow turnip, boiled	4.2	42
Orange Raisin Slaw (see Menu 19)	20.2	56
2½ oz. ice cream	71.2	145
Coffee*—2 t. milk and 1 t. sugar	4.8	33
	183.6	553
Total for Day	341.0	1106

* Decaffeinated coffee may be chosen. It contains 1.7 mg. sodium and 2 calories per cup. With 2 t. milk and 1 t. sugar added, one cup contains 6.5 mg. sodium and 27 calories.

MENU 42

Breakfast	Milligrams Sodium	Calories
4 oz. apricot nectar (½ cup)	2.0	68
¼ cup Instant Ralston (1 oz.) with	.2	110
½ cup milk	58.0	76
Coffee*—2 t. milk and 1 t. sugar	4.8	33
	65.0	287

Lunch		
Spicy Creamed Egg (see Menu 6)	106.5	225
1 mashed potato	4.0	92
Salad—½ sliced apple, ½ sliced grapefruit on		
1 leaf lettuce	5.4	35
Coffee*—2 t. milk and 1 t. sugar	4.8	33
	120.7	385

Dinner		
6 oz. broiled sirloin steak	117.6	300
Baked potato	8.0	96
1 t. butter	.2	38
2 oz. hearts of lettuce	6.8	6
4 t. Vinegar Dressing (see Menu 25)	3.0	19
½ cup apple sauce (4½ oz.)	.4	45
Coffee*—2 t. milk and 1 t. sugar	4.8	33
	140.8	537
Total for Day	326.5	1209

* Decaffeinated coffee may be chosen. It contains 1.7 mg. sodium and 2 calories per cup. With 2 t. milk and 1 t. sugar added, one cup contains 6.5 mg. sodium and 27 calories.

MENU 43

Breakfast	Milligrams Sodium	Calories
1 orange, sliced	2.4	32
1 cup Puffed Rice (½ oz.) with	.1	60
2 oz. blueberries (6 T.) with	.2	30
½ cup milk	58.0	76
1 sl. Low-Sodium Bread (see Menu 1)	3.5	97
Coffee* (without cream or sugar)	—	8
	64.2	303

Lunch		
Curried Egg and Mushrooms (see Menu 7)	78.8	242
1 sl. Low-Sodium Bread (see Menu 1)	3.5	97
Vegetable salad—½ tomato, 1 oz. green pepper, 1 oz. cucumber, 1 oz. lettuce	8.8	22
Coffee* (without cream or sugar)	—	8
	91.1	369

Dinner		
½ lb. Pan-Browned Pork Chops (see Menu 7) with	70.6	304
Creole Sauce (makes 2 portions, one for next day's lunch for spaghetti)	5.0	20
1 baked sweet potato	20.4	92
2½ oz. Candied Carrots (see Menu 7)	68.1	62
½ oz. endive salad (¼ small head) with	2.6	1
4 t. Vinegar Dressing (see Menu 25)	3.0	19
Coffee* (without cream or sugar)	—	8
	169.7	506
Total for Day	325.0	1178

* Decaffeinated coffee may be chosen. It contains 1.7 mg. sodium and 2 calories per cup. With 2 t. milk and 1 t. sugar added, one cup contains 6.5 mg. sodium and 27 calories.

MENU 44

Breakfast	Milligrams Sodium	Calories
4 oz. grapefruit juice (unsweetened)	.4	40
2 T. farina (⅔ oz.—do not use the quick-cooking type) with	.1	67
½ cup milk	58.0	76
Coffee*—2 t. milk and 1 t. sugar	4.8	33
	63.3	216

Lunch		
1 scrambled egg in 1 t. butter	67.2	115
2 oz. spaghetti with	4.4	64
Creole Sauce (made for pork chops on Menu 43)	5.0	20
Salad—½ tomato and 1 oz. lettuce	5.0	11
Coffee*—2 t. milk and 1 t. sugar	4.8	33
	86.4	243

Dinner		
6 oz. grilled calf's liver	188.4	342
1 mashed potato	4.0	92
2½ oz. boiled asparagus (6 spears)	1.2	12
Salad—1 oz. cabbage and 1 oz. pineapple on lettuce	6.9	20
Spicy Baked Apple (see Menu 8)	2.1	152
Coffee*—2 t. milk and 1 t. sugar	4.8	33
	207.4	651
Total for Day	357.1	1110

* Decaffeinated coffee may be chosen. It contains 1.7 mg. sodium and 2 calories per cup. With 2 t. milk and 1 t. sugar added, one cup contains 6.5 mg. sodium and 27 calories.

MENU 45

Breakfast	Milligrams Sodium	Calories
½ grapefruit	.8	12
¼ cup Maltex Cereal	1.0	110
½ cup milk	58.0	76
Coffee*—2 t. milk and 1 t. sugar	4.8	33
	64.6	231

Lunch		
French Omelet (see Menu 9)	67.2	115
Salad—1 oz. cucumber, 1 oz. lettuce, ½ tomato	8.7	14
4 t. Vinegar Dressing (see Menu 25)	3.0	19
1 Hot Roll (see Menu 5)	8.0	77
Coffee* (without cream or sugar)	—	8
	86.9	233

Dinner		
Broiled Flounder (see Menu 17)	146.0	159
1 boiled potato	4.0	92
Fried Eggplant (see Menu 9)	5.8	138
Salad—½ sliced apple, ½ sliced banana, shredded lettuce leaf	5.1	56
Pineapple and Cocoanut (see Menu 3)	3.4	123
Coffee* (without cream or sugar)	—	8
	164.3	576
Total for Day	315.8	1040

* Decaffeinated coffee may be chosen. It contains 1.7 mg. sodium and 2 calories per cup. With 2 t. milk and 1 t. sugar added, one cup contains 6.5 mg. sodium and 27 calories.

MENU 46

Breakfast	Milligrams Sodium	Calories
4 oz. canned pears (2 halves)	9.2	72
1 boiled egg	67.0	77
1 Hot Roll (see Menu 5)	8.0	77
1 t. Butter	.2	38
Coffee*—2 t. milk and 1 t. sugar	4.8	33
	89.2	297

Lunch		
Cucumbers in Sour Cream (see Menu 10)	15.6	129
1 Hot Roll (see Menu 5)	8.0	77
Cantaloupe Gelatin Salad (see Menu 19)	17.4	73
Coffee* (without cream or sugar)	—	8
	41.0	287

Dinner		
Liver Saute (see Menu 34)	125.0	270
1 baked potato with	8.0	96
1 t. butter	.2	38
¼ lb. string beans	3.6	8
Salad—½ apple, ½ grapefruit, lettuce leaf	5.4	35
2¼ oz. ice cream	71.2	145
	213.4	592
Total for Day	343.6	1176

* Decaffeinated coffee may be chosen. It contains 1.7 mg. sodium and 2 calories per cup. With 2 t. milk and 1 t. sugar added, one cup contains 6.5 mg. sodium and 27 calories.

MENU 47

Breakfast	Milligrams Sodium	Calories
Apple Cinnamon Oatmeal*	8.0	145
½ cup low-fat milk	63.7	63
1 sl. Low-Sodium Bread (see Menu 1), toasted, with	3.5	97
1 t. apple butter	—	11
Herb tea	—	—
	75.2	316

Lunch		
10 oz. Black Bean Soup with Wine (see Menu 36)	46.9	277
Very Green Salad (see Menu 23)	20.0	142
2 T. No-Fat Italian Dressing*	3.3	1
½ cup steamed string beans with dash rosemary	3.5	8
Decaffeinated coffee (no cream or sugar)	1.7	2
	75.4	430

Dinner		
1 Pine Nut and Raisin Stuffed Pepper*	11.3	267
¼ cup steamed carrots with sprinkle marjoram	26.1	6
½ cup Coleslaw*	13.3	58
1 Hot Roll (see Menu 5)	8.0	77
Herb tea or	—	—
Decaffeinated coffee (no cream or sugar)	1.7	2
	60.4	410
Total for Day	211.0	1156

* Asterisks denote dishes for which recipes are given.

RECIPES FOR MENU 47

Apple Cinnamon Oatmeal

	Milligrams Sodium	Calories
½ cup and 2 T. water	—	—
¼ cup oatmeal (not instant)	6.7	81
½ cup finely chopped apple, skinned	1.1	20
Sprinkle cinnamon	—	—
1 T. walnut pieces, broken	.2	44
	8.0	145

Place oatmeal in ½ cup cold water. Bring to a boil for a moment. Reduce heat, add apples and walnuts and simmer for about 5 to 7 minutes, stirring frequently. Add cinnamon right before serving.

No-Fat Italian Dressing

Makes ⅔ cup.

	Milligrams Sodium	Calories
⅓ cup red wine vinegar	16.0	3
⅓ cup water	—	—
1 garlic clove, minced	1.7	4
⅛ t. onion powder	—	—
⅛ t. basil	—	—
⅛ t. oregano	—	—
Dash pepper	—	—
Dash paprika	—	—
	17.7	7

One 2-T. serving equals 3.3 mg. sodium and 1 calorie

Mix all ingredients well.

Pine Nut and Raisin Stuffed Peppers

Makes 3 servings.

	Milligrams Sodium	Calories
3 green peppers	12.0	90
⅓ cup raw brown rice	3.7	223
2½ T. olive oil	—	330
½ cup chopped onion	8.0	18
½ cup chopped fresh tomato	2.7	13
2 T. pine nuts	.8	102
1 T. dried raisins (unsulfured)	5.4	25
1 T. chopped fresh parsley	1.2	1
⅛ t. thyme	.2	—
¼ t. oregano	—	—
¼ t. dill	—	—
Pepper to taste	—	—
	34.0	802

One stuffed pepper equals 11.3 mg. sodium and 267 calories

Slice tops from peppers; remove seeds and ribs. Parboil peppers for 5 to 7 minutes until tender. Boil the rice. Saute the onions in the oil. Add the tomato, nuts, raisins and herbs. Season with pepper. Add to the cooked rice. Stuff the peppers with the rice-herb mixture. Pour some water into the baking dish. Cover and cook in a 400° oven for 15 to 20 minutes. Lower heat to 325° for 40 minutes more. Sprinkle with parsley and serve.

Coleslaw

Makes 4 servings.

	Milligrams Sodium	Calories
2 cups finely shredded cabbage	12.6	40
¼ cup shredded carrots	26.1	6
2 T. diced sweet red pepper	.4	3
2 T. low-sodium mayonnaise	12.0	184
Pinch of dry mustard	—	—
1 t. vinegar	1.0	—
⅛ t. pepper	—	—
¼ t. celery seed	1.0	—
	53.1	233

One ½-cup serving equals 13.3 mg. sodium and 58.3 calories

Shred cabbage very finely and cut into 2" strips. Cut the carrot and red pepper. Mix together with cabbage and chill. Sprinkle a little dry mustard into the mayonnaise. Mix with vinegar. Remove vegetables from the refrigerator and sprinkle the celery seed and pepper on the vegetable mixture. Mix in the vinegar and mayonnaise. Serve.

MENU 48

Breakfast	Milligrams Sodium	Calories
1 Shredded Wheat biscuit (1 oz.) with	4.7	103
¼ cup blueberries with	.2	19
½ cup low-fat milk	63.7	63
1 sl. Low-Sodium Bread (see Menu 1) toasted with sprinkle cinnamon	3.5	97
1 t. apple butter	—	11
Herb tea	—	—
	72.1	293

Lunch		
½ cup plus 2 T. Marinated Beans*	9.4	264
1 Hot Roll (see Menu 5)	8.0	77
1 cup steamed broccoli with	10.6	20
2 T. lemon juice	.6	2
Decaffeinated coffee (no cream or sugar)	1.7	2
	30.3	365

Dinner		
4 oz. Almond Cod Tarragon*	126.1	363
¼ of whole Baked Acorn Squash*	2.4	95
Garden Salad (see Menu 12)	23.1	17
2 T. Tarragon Vinegar (see Menu 12)	6.2	1
Herb tea or	—	—
Decaffeinated coffee (no cream or sugar)	1.7	2
	159.5	478
Total for Day	261.9	1136

* Asterisks denote dishes for which recipes are given.

RECIPES FOR MENU 48

Marinated Beans

Makes 4 servings of ½ cup plus 2 T.

	Milligrams Sodium	Calories
1 cup raw kidney beans	20.0	636
½ cup minced onion	8.0	18
3 T. olive oil	—	396
2 T. lemon juice	.6	2
2 T. red wine vinegar	6.0	1
2 T. parsley, freshly chopped	2.5	2
½ t. dried basil	.2	—
½ t. oregano	.2	—
¼ t. onion powder mixed with ½ t. water	.2	
Pepper to taste	—	—
	37.7	1055

One serving of ½ cup plus 2 T. equals 9.4 mg. sodium and 264 calories

Soak the beans overnight. Add the beans slowly to boiling water. Reduce heat immediately and simmer for 2 to 2½ hours. Drain beans. Prepare the marinade by mixing the onion, oil, juice, vinegar and herbs. Add to beans and pepper to taste. Marinate for at least 1 hour before serving.

Almond Cod Tarragon

Makes 2 servings.

Water for steaming fish	—	—
½ lb. cod	248.0	384
1 t. olive oil	—	44
¼ cup slivered almonds	2.0	191
1 T. unsalted butter	1.6	105
2 t. lemon juice	.2	1
¼ t. tarragon	.3	—
	252.1	725

One ¼-lb. serving equals 126.1 mg. sodium and 363 calories

Put fish in steamer. Steam about 1 minute for every ounce of fish, about 8 minutes for ½ pound of fish. Warm olive oil in pan and add slivered almonds. Slowly cook the slivered almonds until they just turn color but not brown. Set aside. Heat the butter until it browns lightly. Squeeze in a few drops of lemon juice and the tarragon. Pour almonds and lemon tarragon butter mixture over fish. Pepper to taste.

Baked Acorn Squash

Makes 4 servings of ¼ squash each.

	Milligrams Sodium	Calories
1 acorn squash	4.0	190
1 T. unsalted butter	.6	114
1½ T. lemon juice	.5	2
2 t. honey	1.5	40
2 T. sherry	3.0	35
Dash nutmeg	—	—
	9.6	381

One serving of ¼ squash equals 2.4 mg. sodium and 95 calories

Scrub squash and cut in half, removing the seeds and fibers. Put the squash in a greased baking dish and pour a little water into the dish. Bake covered in a preheated 350° oven for 30 minutes until partly done. Uncover, adding half of the butter to each half of the squash. Bake uncovered for about 45 minutes more until squash is soft. During the last 15 minutes of cooking time, add a mixture of the lemon juice, honey and sherry to each half and sprinkle with nutmeg.

MENUS 49–60

Less Than 350 Milligrams of Sodium
1800–2200 Calories

MENU 49

Breakfast	Milligrams Sodium	Calories
8 oz. orange juice (1 cup)	4.0	88
¼ cup oatmeal (1 oz.)	9.5	115
½ cup milk	58.0	76
Coffee*—2 t. cream and 1 t. sugar	3.8	65
1 sl. Low-Sodium Bread (see Menu 1)	3.5	97
½ T. marmalade	2.6	37
	81.4	478

Lunch		
Scrambled Eggs and Mushrooms (see Menu 1)	81.1	130
Salad—½ grapefruit, 1 oz. lettuce	4.2	15
3 canned prunes (3⅓ oz.)	2.8	100
1 sl. Low-Sodium Bread (see Menu 1)	3.5	97
1 t. butter (unsalted)	.2	38
Coffee*—2 t. cream and 1 t. sugar	3.8	65
	95.6	445

Dinner		
6 oz. broiled liver	146.4	246
4 oz. boiled peas	—	56
1 boiled potato with	4.0	92
1 t. butter (unsalted)	.2	38
Salad—½ sliced banana, ½ sliced apple, 1 leaf lettuce	5.1	56
1 T. French Dressing (see Menu 3)	—	88
Apple Pie—⅛ sl. (see Menu 4)	2.9	388
Coffee*—2 t. cream and 1 t. sugar	3.8	65
	162.4	1029
Total for Day	339.4	1952

* Decaffeinated coffee may be chosen. It contains 1.7 mg. sodium and 2 calories per cup. With 2 t. milk and 1 t. sugar added, one cup contains 6.5 mg. sodium and 27 calories.

MENU 50

Breakfast	Milligrams Sodium	Calories
4 oz. orange juice and ½ sliced banana	2.5	77
1 T. rice (cooked)	1.2	68
½ cup milk, hot	58.0	76
1 t. sugar and cinnamon may be added to milk	—	19
1 sl. Low-Sodium Bread (see Menu 1)	3.5	97
2 t. jelly	4.8	49
Coffee*—2 t. cream and 1 t. sugar	3.8	65
	73.8	451

Lunch		
1 Fried Egg and Mashed Potato (see Menu 2)	72.8	249
4 oz. boiled fresh asparagus with	2.0	20
1 T. melted butter	.7	113
1 sl. Low-Sodium Bread	3.5	97
1 cup fruit salad, canned (4 oz.)	10.0	80
Coffee*—2 t. cream and 1 t. sugar	3.8	65
	92.8	624

Dinner		
½ grapefruit	.8	12
½ lb. broiled shoulder lamb chops, lean only (weighed with fat and bone)	136.0	288
4 oz. boiled peas	—	56
1 boiled parsley potato	4.0	92
Salad—1 oz. cucumber, ½ tomato and 1 oz. lettuce	8.7	14
4 t. Vinegar Dressing (see Menu 1)	3.0	63
Cantaloupe Gelatin Salad with French Dressing for Fruit Salad (see Menu 19)	18.6	181
Coffee*—2 t. cream and 1 t. sugar	3.8	65
	174.9	771
Total for Day	341.5	1846

* Decaffeinated coffee may be chosen. It contains 1.7 mg. sodium and 2 calories per cup. With 2 t. milk and 1 t. sugar added, one cup contains 6.5 mg. sodium and 27 calories.

MENU 51

Breakfast	Milligrams Sodium	Calories
Mix 4 oz. orange and 4 oz. grapefruit juice	2.4	84
1 Shredded Wheat biscuit (1 oz.) with	4.7	103
½ banana (2½ oz.) with	.7	55
½ cup milk	58.0	76
1 sl. Low-Sodium Bread (see Menu 1)	3.5	97
1 t. butter (unsalted)	.2	38
Coffee*—2 t. cream and 1 t. sugar	3.8	65
	73.3	518

Lunch		
Spanish Omelet (see Menu 3)	93.0	136
1 sl. Low-Sodium Bread	3.5	97
1 t. butter	.2	38
Nut and Apple Tapioca (see Menu 3)	8.5	357
Coffee*—2 t. cream and 1 t. sugar	3.8	65
	109.0	693

Dinner		
Broiled Flounder (see Menu 17)	146.0	159
Baked potato with 1 t. butter	8.2	134
Fried Eggplant (see Menu 9)	5.8	138
Hearts of lettuce (2 oz.)	6.8	6
1 T. French Dressing (see Menu 3)	—	88
Pineapple and Cocoanut (see Menu 3)	3.4	123
Coffee*—2 t. cream and 1 t. sugar	3.8	65
	174.0	713
Total for Day	356.3	1924

* Decaffeinated coffee may be chosen. It contains 1.7 mg. sodium and 2 calories per cup. With 2 t. milk and 1 t. sugar added, one cup contains 6.5 mg. sodium and 27 calories.

MENU 52

Breakfast	Milligrams Sodium	Calories
8 oz. orange juice	4.0	88
1 cup Puffed Rice (½ oz.)	.1	60
½ cup milk	58.0	76
1 sl. Low-Sodium Bread (see Menu 1)	3.5	97
1 t. butter	.2	38
Coffee*—2 t. cream and 1 t. sugar	3.8	65
	69.6	424

Lunch		
Mushroom Omelet (see Menu 4)	73.8	127
2 oz. lettuce and ½ tomato	8.4	14
1 t. French Dressing (see Menu 3)	—	88
1 sl. Low-Sodium Bread	3.5	97
1 t. butter	.2	38
Coffee*—2 t. cream and 1 t. sugar	3.8	65
	89.7	429

Dinner		
½ grapefruit with 1 t. honey	2.3	39
Beef Stew (⅔ of recipe for today, ⅓ for tomorrow's lunch; see Menu 4)	151.4	386
1 sl. Low-Sodium Bread	3.5	97
Endive salad (¼ small head)	2.6	1
1 T. French Dressing (see Menu 3)	—	88
Nut and Apple Tapioca (see Menu 3)	8.5	357
Coffee*—2 t. cream and 1 t. sugar	3.8	65
	172.1	1033
Total for Day	331.4	1886

* Decaffeinated coffee may be chosen. It contains 1.7 mg. sodium and 2 calories per cup. With 2 t. milk and 1 t. sugar added, one cup contains 6.5 mg. sodium and 27 calories.

MENU 53

Breakfast	Milligrams Sodium	Calories
8 oz. pineapple juice	.8	144
1 cup Puffed Wheat (½ oz.)	.4	55
½ banana cut into cereal (2 oz.)	.6	44
½ cup milk	58.0	76
1 Hot Roll (see Menu 5)	8.0	77
1 t. butter	.2	38
Coffee*—2 t. cream and 1 t. sugar	3.8	65
	71.8	499

Lunch		
Beef Stew (left over from yesterday's dinner on Menu 52)	76.0	193
1 Hot Roll	8.0	77
1 t. butter	.2	38
Salad—½ orange, 2 oz. lettuce	8.0	22
1 T. French Dressing (see Menu 3)	—	88
4 oz. canned peaches (2 halves)	6.8	76
Coffee*—2 t. cream and 1 t. sugar	3.8	65
	102.8	559

Dinner		
Macaroni with Liver (see Menu 14)	79.6	231
4 oz. Pan-Fried Potatoes (see Menu 5)	8.0	316
4 oz. Brussels Sprouts (see Menu 5)	9.1	69
Salad—½ oz. cucumber, 1 oz. lettuce, ½ tomato, ½ oz. green pepper	6.8	16
Custard Cake Pudding (see Menu 5)	64.2	319
Coffee*—2 t. cream and 1 t. sugar	3.8	65
	171.5	1016
Total for Day	346.1	2074

* Decaffeinated coffee may be chosen. It contains 1.7 mg. sodium and 2 calories per cup. With 2 t. milk and 1 t. sugar added, one cup contains 6.5 mg. sodium and 27 calories.

MENU 54

Breakfast	Milligrams Sodium	Calories
8 oz. apricot nectar	4.0	136
¼ cup Instant Ralston (1 oz.) with	.2	110
½ cup milk with	58.0	76
1 T. raisins	5.0	23
1 sl. Low-Sodium Bread (see Menu 1)	3.5	97
1 t. butter	.2	38
Coffee*—2 t. cream and 1 t. sugar	3.8	65
	74.7	545

Lunch

Spicy Creamed Egg (see Menu 6)	106.5	225
1 mashed potato	4.0	92
Salad—½ sliced apple, ½ sliced grapefruit on		
1 leaf lettuce	5.4	35
Peach Cocktail (see Menu 6)	6.0	99
Coffee*—2 t. cream and 1 t. sugar	3.8	65
	125.7	516

Dinner

6 oz. broiled sirloin steak	117.6	300
1 baked potato	8.0	96
1 t. butter	.2	38
4 oz. boiled peas	4.0	56
2 oz. hearts of lettuce	6.8	6
1 T. French Dressing (see Menu 3)	—	88
Banana and Grape Gelatin (see Menu 20)	2.4	106
Coffee*—2 t. cream and 1 t. sugar	3.8	65
	142.8	755
Total for Day	343.2	1816

* Decaffeinated coffee may be chosen. It contains 1.7 mg. sodium and 2 calories per cup. With 2 t. milk and 1 t. sugar added, one cup contains 6.5 mg. sodium and 27 calories.

MENU 55

Breakfast	Milligrams Sodium	Calories
1 orange, sliced	2.4	32
1 cup Puffed Rice (½ oz.) with	.1	60
2 oz. blueberries with	.2	30
½ cup milk	58.0	76
1 sl. Low-Sodium Bread, toasted (see Menu 1)	3.5	97
1 t. butter	.2	38
1 T. marmalade	5.2	74
Coffee*—2 t. cream and 1 t. sugar	3.8	65
	73.4	472

Lunch		
Curried Egg and Mushrooms (see Menu 7)	78.8	242
1 sl. Low-Sodium Bread	3.5	97
1 t. butter	.2	38
Vegetable salad—½ tomato, 1 oz. lettuce, 1 oz. green pepper, 1 oz. cucumber	8.8	22
Coffee*—2 t. cream and 1 t. sugar	3.8	65
3 Seed Cookies (see Menu 7)	12.0	255
	107.1	719

Dinner		
½ lb. Pan-Broiled Pork Chops (see Menu 7) with	70.6	304
Creole Sauce (makes 2 portions, one for next day's lunch for spaghetti)	5.0	20
1 baked potato with 1 t. butter	8.2	134
2½ oz. Candied Carrots (see Menu 7)	68.1	62
½ oz. endive salad (¼ small head) with	2.6	1
1 T. French Dressing (see Menu 3)	—	88
Coffee*—2 t. cream and 1 t. sugar	3.8	65
2 Seed Cookies	8.0	170
	166.3	844
Total for Day	346.8	2035

* Decaffeinated coffee may be chosen. It contains 1.7 mg. sodium and 2 calories per cup. With 2 t. milk and 1 t. sugar added, one cup contains 6.5 mg. sodium and 27 calories.

MENU 56

Breakfast	Milligrams Sodium	Calories
4 oz. grapefruit juice (unsweetened)	.4	40
2 T. farina (⅔ oz.—do not use quick-cooking type)	.1	67
½ cup milk	58.0	76
1 sl. Low-Sodium Bread (see Menu 1)	3.5	97
1 t. butter	.2	38
Coffee*—2 t. cream and 1 t. sugar	3.8	65
	66.0	383

Lunch		
1 scrambled egg in 1 t. butter	67.2	115
2 oz. spaghetti with	4.4	64
Creole Sauce (made for pork chops for previous day's dinner)	5.0	20
Coffee*—2 t. cream and 1 t. sugar	3.8	65
2 Sugar Cookies (see Menu 8)	.6	136
	81.0	400

Dinner		
6 oz. grilled calf's liver	188.4	342
1 mashed potato with	4.0	92
1 t. butter	.2	38
4 oz. green peas with 1 t. butter	.6	94
Salad—½ apple, ½ sliced grapefruit on 1 oz. lettuce	5.4	35
French Dressing for Fruit Salad (see Menu 19)	1.2	108
Spicy Baked Apple (see Menu 8)	2.1	152
Coffee*—2 t. cream and 1 t. sugar	3.8	65
2 Sugar Cookies	.6	136
	206.3	1062
Total for Day	353.3	1845

* Decaffeinated coffee may be chosen. It contains 1.7 mg. sodium and 2 calories per cup. With 2 t. milk and 1 t. sugar added, one cup contains 6.5 mg. sodium and 27 calories.

MENU 57

Breakfast	Milligrams Sodium	Calories
½ grapefruit	.8	12
¼ cup Maltex Wheat Cereal (1 oz.)	1.0	110
2 canned prunes (2 oz.)	1.7	60
½ cup milk	58.0	76
1 Hot Roll (see Menu 5)	8.0	77
1 t. butter	.2	38
Coffee*—2 t. cream and 1 t. sugar	3.8	65
	73.5	438

Lunch		
French Omelet (see Menu 9)	67.2	115
1 boiled potato with	4.0	92
1 t. butter	.2	38
Salad—1 oz. cucumber, 1 oz. lettuce, ½ tomato	8.7	14
1 T. French Dressing (see Menu 3)	—	88
Pineapple and Cocoanut (see Menu 3)	3.4	123
Coffee*—2 t. cream and 1 t. sugar	3.8	65
	87.3	535

Dinner		
Broiled Flounder (see Menu 17)	146.0	159
1 boiled potato	4.0	92
Fried Eggplant (see Menu 9)	5.8	138
Salad—½ sliced apple, ½ sliced banana, 1 shredded lettuce leaf	5.1	56
French Dressing for Fruit Salad (see Menu 19)	1.2	108
Coffee Mousse (see Menu 21)	31.4	406
Coffee*—2 t. cream and 1 t. sugar	3.8	65
	197.3	1024
Total for Day	358.1	1997

* Decaffeinated coffee may be chosen. It contains 1.7 mg. sodium and 2 calories per cup. With 2 t. milk and 1 t. sugar added, one cup contains 6.5 mg. sodium and 27 calories.

MENU 58

Breakfast	Milligrams Sodium	Calories
4 oz. canned pears (2 halves)	9.2	72
¼ cup Wheatena (1 oz.)	.2	110
½ cup milk (hot) spiced with	58.0	76
1 t. sugar and bit of cinnamon	—	18
1 Hot Roll (see Menu 5)	8.0	77
2 t. butter	.4	76
Coffee*—2 t. cream and 1 t. sugar	3.8	65
	79.6	494

Lunch		
Cucumbers in Sour Cream (see Menu 10)	15.6	119
1 Hot Roll	8.0	77
1 t. butter	.2	38
Cantaloupe Gelatin Salad (see Menu 19)	17.4	73
French Dressing for Fruit Salad (see Menu 19)	6.2	108
Coffee*—2 t. cream and 1 t. sugar	3.8	65
	46.2	480

Dinner		
4 oz. Liver Saute (see Menu 34)	125.0	270
1 baked potato with	8.0	96
1 t. butter	.2	38
¼ lb. string beans with	3.6	8
1 t. butter	.2	38
Salad—½ apple, ½ sliced grapefruit on 1 lettuce leaf	5.4	35
French Dressing for Fruit Salad (see Menu 19)	1.2	108
Sweet Pilau (see Menu 17)	25.8	459
Coffee*—2 t. cream and 1 t. sugar	3.8	65
	173.2	1117
Total for Day	299.0	2091

* Decaffeinated coffee may be chosen. It contains 1.7 mg. sodium and 2 calories per cup. With 2 t. milk and 1 t. sugar added, one cup contains 6.5 mg. sodium and 27 calories.

MENU 59

Breakfast	Milligrams Sodium	Calories
8 oz. pineapple juice	2.2	144
1 cup Puffed Wheat with	.4	55
½ banana (2½ oz.) with	.7	55
½ cup low-fat milk	63.7	63
Herb tea or	—	—
Decaffeinated coffee (no cream or sugar)	1.7	2
	68.7	319

Lunch		
1 cup Minestrone Soup (see Menu 23)	40.6	172
1⅓ cups Italian Zucchini Salad, chilled (see Menu 11)	45.3	243
1 Steamed Artichoke*	58.7	325
2 sls. Herb Toast (see Menu 11)	7.4	270
Herb tea (without caffeine)	—	—
	152.0	1010

Dinner		
4 oz. Chicken Curry*	93.8	181
¾ cup Indian Green Beans*	7.3	33
1 Hot Roll (see Menu 5)	8.0	77
1 t. unsalted butter	.2	38
¼ cup long grain brown rice, cooked	2.8	167
Sprinkle of turmeric for rice	—	—
Decaffeinated coffee (no cream or sugar)	1.7	2
	113.8	498
Total for Day	334.5	1827

* Asterisks denote dishes for which recipes are given.

RECIPES FOR MENU 59

Steamed Artichoke

	Milligrams Sodium	Calories
1 artichoke	57.0	57
¼ cup water	—	—
2 T. olive oil	—	264
1 garlic clove, minced	1.7	4
Sprinkle black pepper	—	—
	58.7	325

Steam artichoke until tender. Saute garlic in olive oil. Place quartered steamed artichoke in pan. Cook for 2 minutes in the oil. Remove and season with fresh ground pepper.

Chicken Curry

Makes 3 servings.

¾ lb. skinned breast meat (not weighed with rest of chicken)	275.4	412
1 T. vegetable oil	—	122
¼ cup finely minced onion	4.0	10
2 t. curry powder	2.0	—
1 cup water	—	—
	281.4	544

One ¼-lb. serving equals 93.8 mg. sodium and 181 calories

Saute onions in vegetable oil. Add the curry powder. Finally add the chicken and cook until almost dry. Then add 1 cup of water, covering and simmering for about 1½ hours until chicken is tender and sauce thickens.

Indian Green Beans

Makes 2 servings.

	Milligrams Sodium	Calories
1½ cups string beans	10.5	24
¼ cup sliced onion	2.9	7
4 T. water	—	—
1 t. unsalted butter	.2	38
1 t. chopped fresh ginger root	.5	—
⅛ t. ground fennel seed	.2	—
	14.6	69

One serving equals 7.3 mg. sodium and 35 calories

Slice beans slantwise. Cut onions into the same ½" slivers. Boil 4 T. or so of water and add the butter. Add the beans, onions and ginger root. Sprinkle in the ground fennel seed, mixing well. Cover the pot, letting it steam for 5 to 7 minutes. Serve very hot. A vegetable steamer may also be used to prepare this dish. Be sure not to overcook the beans, whichever method is used.

MENU 60

Breakfast	Milligrams Sodium	Calories
4 oz. apricot nectar (½ cup)	2.0	68
Walnut Apricot Oatmeal* with	17.0	201
½ cup low-fat milk	63.7	63
1 sl. Low-Sodium Bread, toasted (see Menu 1)	3.5	97
1 t. unsalted butter	.2	38
Herb tea or	—	—
Decaffeinated coffee (no cream or sugar)	1.7	2
	88.1	469

Lunch		
1 cup Pasta e Fagioli (see Menu 12)	18.9	316
1 sl. Parmesan Toast (see Menu 23)	41.7	155
¾ cup Herbed Steamed Zucchini*	4.3	161
Very Green Salad (see Menu 23)	20.0	142
1 T. Tarragon Vinegar and Oil Dressing (see Menu 23)	1.5	89
Herb tea (without caffeine)	—	—
	86.4	863

Dinner		
4 oz. Tasty Wine Chicken*	97.2	237
1 Basil Baked Tomato*	6.0	75
¼ cup raw long grain brown rice, cooked	2.8	167
Sprinkle oregano for rice	—	—
Garden Salad (see Menu 12)	23.1	17
2 T. Avocado Dressing*	.7	118
Decaffeinated coffee (no cream or sugar)	1.7	2
	131.5	616
Total for Day	306.0	1948

* Asterisks denote dishes for which recipes are given.

RECIPES FOR MENU 60

Walnut Apricot Oatmeal

	Milligrams Sodium	Calories
¼ cup regular oatmeal (not instant)	6.7	81
½ cup plus 2 T. water	—	—
5 dried apricot halves (unsulfured)	9.8	32
2 T. walnut pieces, broken	.5	88
	17.0	201

Place oatmeal in cold water. Bring to a boil for a moment. Reduce heat, add dried apricots and walnuts and simmer for 5 to 7 minutes, stirring frequently.

Herbed Steamed Zucchini

¾ cup zucchini, sliced	.5	20
1 T. olive oil	—	132
2 T. minced onion	2.0	5
1 clove garlic, minced	1.7	4
¼ t. basil	.1	—
⅛ t. oregano	—	—
Sprinkle pepper	—	—
	4.3	161

Cut zucchini in rounds without peeling. Steam for about 10 minutes or until tender. Saute the onion and garlic in olive oil briefly. Add the cooked zucchini and cook for 1 minute more. Sprinkle with herbs and pepper to taste. Serve hot.

Basil Baked Tomatoes

Makes 2 servings.

	Milligrams Sodium	Calories
2 medium tomatoes	8.7	41
1 T. chopped fresh parsley	1.3	—
2 t. wheat germ	—	16
2 t. olive oil	—	88
1 garlic clove, minced	1.7	4
½ t. basil	.2	—
Pepper to taste	—	—
	11.9	149

One serving of 1 tomato equals 6.0 mg. sodium and 75 calories

Cut off the top of each tomato. Place tomatoes on oiled baking sheet. Mix the wheat germ, parsley, garlic and seasonings and sprinkle on top of tomatoes. Sprinkle with olive oil, cover and bake in a preheated 375° oven for 30 minutes.

Tasty Wine Chicken

Makes 3 servings.

¾ lb. skinned chicken breast meat (not weighed with rest of chicken)	275.4	412
2 T. vegetable oil	—	244
¼ cup dry white wine	12.2	44
2 T. finely minced onion	2.0	5
1 garlic clove, minced	1.7	4
⅛ t. thyme	.2	—
⅛ t. tarragon	.1	—
⅛ t. rosemary	—	—
¼ t. black pepper	—	—
	291.6	709

One ¼-lb. serving equals 97.2 mg. sodium and 237 calories

Mix the herbs, wine and oil and chill for several hours. Pour over chicken and marinate for 3 hours more in the refrigerator. Broil 5 to 6 inches from the heat, basting each side for 15 to 20 minutes with the marinade mixture.

Avocado Dressing

Makes 2 servings.

	Milligrams Sodium	Calories
¼ of a ripe avocado, mashed	1.0	112
1 T. lemon juice	.3	1
1 T. vegetable oil	—	122
Sprinkle garlic powder	—	—
Sprinkle pepper	—	—
	1.3	235

One 2-T. serving equals .7 mg. sodium and 118 calories

Mash ripe avocado, adding the lemon juice and vegetable oil. Add garlic powder and pepper to taste.

LOW-SODIUM DIET FOR THE PERSON WHO EATS OUT

If obliged to have lunch or dinner out, the patient is faced with rather a difficult problem. He will be obliged to limit his menu to more or less the same type of food each day. A few sample meals which may be obtained in a restaurant follow. (Parenthesis signifies amount is variable.)

MENU A

	Milligrams Sodium	Calories
½ grapefruit	.8	12
2 boiled eggs	134.4	154
Salad—2 oz. lettuce, ½ tomato	8.0	14
Dressing—vinegar and sugar	3.0	19
Coffee*—2 t. cream and 1 t. sugar	3.8	65
Baked apple	2.4	59
	152.4	323

MENU B

	Milligrams Sodium	Calories
8 oz. steak (broiled)	156.8	400
1 baked potato (1 t. butter, unsalted)	8.2	134
Salad—No dressing except vinegar, sugar, and oil	(11.0)	(33)
2½ oz. ice cream	71.2	145
Coffee*—2 t. cream and 1 t. sugar	3.8	65
	251.0	777

MENU C

	Milligrams Sodium	Calories
Fruit cup	5.0	40
4 oz. lamb chops, broiled	103.6	212
Baked potato (1 t. butter, unsalted)	8.2	134
Salad—No dressing except vinegar or sugar and oil	(11.0)	(33)
Canned pineapple	1.4	90
Coffee*—2 t. cream and 1 t. sugar	3.8	65
	133.0	574

* Decaffeinated coffee may be chosen. it contains 1.7 mg. sodium and 2 calories per cup. With 2 t. milk and 1 t. sugar added, one cup contains 6.5 mg. sodium and 27 calories.

MENU D

	Milligrams Sodium	Calories
½ lb. broiled liver	195.2	328
1 baked potato	8.0	96
Salad—No dressing except vinegar or sugar and oil	(11.0)	(33)
1 cup fruit salad (may be canned)	10.0	80
Coffee*—2 t. cream and 1 t. sugar	3.8	65
	228.0	602

MENU E

	Milligrams Sodium	Calories
½ grapefruit	.8	12
½ lb. broiled lamb chops (shoulder)	136.0	288
1 baked potato (1 t. butter, unsalted)	8.2	134
Salad—No dressing except vinegar, sugar or oil	(11.0)	(33)
4 oz. canned peaches (or other fruit)	6.8	76
Coffee*—2 t. cream and 1 t. sugar	3.8	65
	166.6	608

The secret of eating out lies in the use of Jewish unleavened bread, called matzoh. This is a tasty and satisfying substitute for bread. However, be sure to buy the plain matzoh marked "Passover," which is traditionally made without salt.

Tea matzoh, which contains slightly more sodium than the Passover matzoh, will be found to be a very pleasant variation.

Care must be taken, however, to avoid such preparations as poppy seed matzohs, tasty wafer matzohs and whole wheat matzohs, as well as matzohs, American-style.

* Decaffeinated coffee may be chosen. It contains 1.7 mg. sodium and 2 calories per cup. With 2 t. milk and 1 t. sugar added, one cup contains 6.5 mg. sodium and 27 calories.

THE SALT-FREE DIET FOR THE DIABETIC

One of the most frequent complications of diabetes is arteriosclerotic vascular disease. Adequate diets are available to the person with uncomplicated diabetes. The diabetic, however, who suffers from hypertension requires the special type of sodium-free diet suggested in this book. It is, of course, expected that he will not attempt self-treatment, but will consult with his physician in the selection of the diet best suited to him.

All fruits must be water packed.
No salt is to be added to any food.
Cream to be used should be 20 percent.
All canned foods must be salt-free.
When coffee appears in the menus, decaffeinated coffee may be substituted. It contains 1.7 mg. sodium and 2 calories per cup.

There may be slight variations between the calories listed on the Diabetic Salt-Free Diet and the ones preceding. This slight difference is due to our use of Food and Beverage Analysis by Bridges and Mattice for our authority on analysis for the Diabetic Menus.

SUMMARY OF THE MENUS AND THEIR VALUES

Menu	Carb.	Prot.	Fats	Cal.	Mg. na.
A	127.0	68.2	68.3	1436	358.3
B	128.8	66.2	78.8	1536	324.9
C	135.3	63.9	76.2	1530	262.4
D	149.7	73.7	83.7	1683	319.1
E	160.3	77.4	92.5	1823	376.8
F	147.5	75.7	85.8	1723	320.0
G	140.0	90.7	98.1	1821	423.2
H	185.3	79.7	99.4	2037	409.6
I	199.8	99.3	90.7	2051	415.0

MENU A

	Carb.	Prot.	Fat	Cal.	Mg. Na.
Breakfast					
4 oz. canned pears, water-packed (2 halves)	4.9	.4	.1	25	8.8
¼ cup Wheatena (1 oz.)	21.7	3.2	.8	110	.2
½ cup milk	6.0	3.9	4.8	85	58.0
1 sl. Low-Sodium Bread (Menu 1)	18.2	2.9	1.5	101	3.5
2 t. butter	—	—	5.6	54	.4
Coffee with 1 T. cream	2.3	.9	3.0	39	5.7
	53.1	11.3	15.8	414	76.6
Lunch					
1 sliced hard-boiled egg on	—	6.7	5.2	75	67
2 oz. lettuce	.5	.6	.2	6	6.8
Cucumbers in Sour Cream (Menu 10)	4.7	1.2	6.0	77	15.6
Coffee with 1 T. cream	2.3	.9	3.0	39	5.7
	7.5	9.4	14.4	197	95.1
Dinner					
8 oz. steak, broiled (fat not to be eaten)	—	33.9	6.9	205	156.8
1 baked potato (5 oz.)	38.1	4.6	.1	175	10
1 t. butter	—	—	2.8	27	.2
¾ cup string beans (2½ oz.)	5.8	1.8	.2	35	4.5
2 t. butter	—	—	5.6	54	.2
Salad—½ apple, ½ sliced grapefruit on lettuce leaf, with	11.6	1.1	.3	55	6.0
3 chopped walnuts	1.8	4.8	9.8	117	.4
1 T. French Dressing (Menu 3)	.4	—	9.3	88	—
3 prunes, water-packed	6.4	.4	.1	30	2.8
Coffee with 1 T. cream	2.3	.9	3.0	39	5.7
	66.4	47.5	38.1	825	186.6
Total for Day	127.0	68.2	68.3	1436	358.3

MENU B

	Carb.	Prot.	Fat	Cal.	Mg. Na.
Breakfast					
1 orange, sliced	8.5	.8	.2	40	2.4
1 cup Puffed Rice (½ oz.) with	13.3	.9	—	60	.1
2 oz. blueberries, with	5.4	.2	.2	25	.2
½ cup milk	6.0	3.9	4.8	85	58.0
1 t. butter	—	—	2.8	27	.2
1 sl. Low-Sodium Bread (Menu 1)	18.2	2.9	1.5	101	3.5
Coffee with 1 T. cream	2.3	.9	3.0	39	5.7
	53.7	9.6	12.5	377	70.1
Lunch					
Curried Egg and Mushrooms (Menu 7)	3.1	7.9	14.0	174	78.8
1 t. butter	—	—	2.8	27	.2
1 sl. Low-Sodium Bread (Menu 1)	18.2	2.9	1.5	101	3.5
Vegetable salad—½ tomato, 1 oz. green pepper, 1 oz. cucumber, 1 oz. lettuce	3.7	1.3	.3	24	8.8
½ cup pineapple (water-packed) with	7.6	.2	—	32	1.2
6 soft-shell walnuts, chopped	4.7	5.8	22.2	250	.6
Coffee with 1 T. cream	2.3	.9	3.0	39	5.7
	39.6	19.0	43.8	647	98.8
Dinner					
½ lb. Pan-Browned Pork Chops (Menu 7) with	—	32.9	8.3	215	70.6
Creole Sauce (Menu 7)	4.5	1.0	.4	26	5.0
1 boiled potato, sprinkled with parsley	18.0	2.2	.1	85	4.0
2½ oz. Candied Carrots (Menu 7)	9.7	.4	1.4	56	68.1
½ oz. endive salad	.6	.2	—	3	2.6
1 T. French Dressing (Menu 3)	.4	—	9.3	88	—
Coffee with 1 T. cream	2.3	.9	3.0	39	5.7
	35.5	37.6	22.5	512	156.0
Total for Day	128.8	66.2	78.8	1536	324.9

	Carb.	Prot.	Fat	Cal.	Mg. Na.
Breakfast					
4 oz. canned pears, water-packed (2 halves)	4.9	.4	.1	25	8.8
1/4 cup Wheatena (1 oz.)	21.7	3.2	.8	110	.2
1/2 cup milk	6.0	3.9	4.8	85	58.0
1 sl. Low-Sodium Bread (Menu 1)	18.2	2.9	1.5	101	3.5
1 t. butter	—	—	2.8	27	.2
Coffee with 1 T. cream	2.3	.9	3.0	39	5.7
	53.1	11.3	13.0	387	76.4
Lunch					
Cucumbers in Sour Cream (Menu 10)	4.7	1.2	6.0	77	15.6
1 sl. Low-Sodium Bread (Menu 1)	18.2	2.9	1.5	101	3.5
1 t. butter	—	—	2.8	27	.2
Cantaloupe Gelatin Salad (Menu 19)—Add 6 soft-shelled walnuts, chopped fine, to the recipe	26.4	7.7	22.4	350	18.2
Coffee with 1 T. cream	2.3	.9	3.0	39	5.7
	51.6	12.7	35.7	594	43.2
Dinner					
4 oz. Liver Saute (Menu 34)	9.7	34.3	18.1	351	125.0
6 stalks boiled asparagus (2½ oz.)	1.2	1.8	.3	15	1.2
1 t. butter	—	—	2.8	27	.2
3/4 cup string beans (2½ oz.) with	5.8	1.8	.2	35	4.5
1 t. butter	—	—	2.8	27	.2
Salad—1/2 apple, 1/2 sliced grapefruit on lettuce leaf	11.6	1.1	.3	55	6.0
Coffee with 1 T. cream	2.3	.9	3.0	39	5.7
	30.6	39.9	37.5	549	142.8
Total for Day	135.3	63.9	76.2	1530	262.4

MENU D

	Carb.	Prot.	Fat	Cal.	Mg. Na.
Breakfast					
½ small cantaloupe (7 oz.)	10.0	—	—	40	26.6
1 cup Puffed Wheat (½ oz.)	11.3	2.3	.2	55	.4
½ banana cut into cereal	13.1	.8	.4	60	.7
4 T. cream (20%)	2.3	1.7	12.0	124	22.8
1 sl. Low-Sodium Bread (Menu 1)	18.2	2.9	1.5	101	3.5
1 t. butter	—	—	2.8	27	.2
Coffee with 1 T. cream	2.3	.9	3.0	39	5.7
	57.2	8.6	19.9	446	59.9
Lunch					
Curried Egg and Mushrooms (Menu 7)	3.1	7.9	14.0	174	78.8
1 sl. Low-Sodium Bread (Menu 1)	18.2	2.9	1.5	101	3.5
1 t. butter	—	—	2.8	27	.2
Salad—½ tomato, 1 oz. lettuce, 1 oz. green pepper, 1 oz. cucumber	3.7	1.3	.3	24	8.8
8 cashew nuts, fried in coconut oil, unsalted	2.0	4.3	7.9	100	1.8
Coffee with 1 T. cream	2.3	.9	3.0	39	5.7
	29.3	17.3	29.5	465	98.8
Dinner					
½ lb. broiled shoulder lamb chops	—	35.6	8.6	225	136.0
1 baked potato, 5 oz., with	38.1	4.6	.1	175	10.0
1 t. butter	—	—	2.8	27	.2
Salad—½ orange, 2 oz. lettuce, 3 walnuts	6.4	5.8	10.1	143	7.8
1 T. French Dressing (Menu 3)	.4	—	9.3	88	—
8 oz. watermelon, 1 cup diced	16.0	.9	.4	75	.7
Coffee with 1 T. cream	2.3	.9	3.0	39	5.7
	63.2	47.8	34.3	772	160.4
Total for Day	149.7	73.7	83.7	1683	319.1

MENU E

	Carb.	Prot.	Fat	Cal.	Mg. Na.
Breakfast					
4 oz. orange juice	11.3	.7	—	50	2.0
1 Shredded Wheat biscuit with	24.5	3.3	.5	120	4.7
½ banana (2½ oz.) with	13.1	.8	.4	60	.7
½ cup milk	6.0	3.9	4.8	85	58.0
1 sl. Low-Sodium Bread (Menu 1)	18.2	2.9	1.5	101	3.5
1 t. butter	—	—	2.8	27	.2
Coffee with 1 T. cream	2.3	.9	3.0	39	5.7
	75.4	12.5	13.0	482	74.8
Lunch					
Spanish Omelet (Menu 3)	9.5	9.9	5.8	130	93.0
1 sl. Low-Sodium Bread (Menu 1)	18.2	2.9	1.5	101	3.5
1 t. butter	—	—	2.8	27	.2
Coffee with 1 T. cream	2.3	.9	3.0	39	5.7
	30.0	13.7	13.1	297	102.4
Dinner					
Broiled Flounder (Menu 17)	1.5	32.7	4.2	178	146.0
4 oz. Pan-Fried Potatoes (Menu 5)	22.0	2.8	24.1	322	8.0
Diced Carrots with Minted Peas (Menu 3)	9.6	3.8	1.7	73	28.9
Hearts of lettuce (2 oz.)	.5	.6	.2	6	6.8
1 T. French Dressing (Menu 3)	.4	—	9.3	88	
Pineapple and Cocoanut (Menu 3)	18.6	10.4	23.9	338	4.2
Coffee with 1 T. cream	2.3	.9	3.0	39	5.7
	54.9	51.2	66.4	1044	199.6
Total for Day	160.3	77.4	92.5	1823	376.8

MENU F

Breakfast	Carb.	Prot.	Fat	Cal.	Mg. Na.
8 oz. orange juice	22.6	1.4	—	100	4.0
1/4 cup oatmeal (2/3 oz.)	13.5	3.2	1.4	80	6.3
4 T. cream (20%)	2.3	1.7	12.0	124	22.8
Coffee with 1 T. cream	2.3	.9	3.0	39	5.7
1 sl. Low-Sodium Bread (Menu 1)	18.2	2.9	1.5	101	3.5
1 t. butter	—	—	2.8	27	.2
	58.9	10.1	20.7	471	42.5

Lunch

Scrambled Egg and Mushrooms (Menu 1): Substitute 1 T.

cream for the milk in the recipe	.6	7.1	11.0	133	76.8
Salad—1/2 apple, 1/2 banana, 1 lettuce leaf	19.4	1.3	.7	90	5.1

Orange Rice Custard (Menu 1): Substitute saccharine for

sugar in the recipe	20.6	3.6	15.1	270	30.6
	40.6	12.0	26.8	493	112.5

Dinner

6 oz. broiled liver	4.3	35.2	9.3	232	146.4
2 1/2 oz. boiled peas	8.0	4.3	.4	55	.5
1 boiled potato (3 1/3 oz.)	18.0	2.2	.1	85	4.0
2 t. butter	—	—	5.6	54	.4
Salad—1/2 grapefruit, 1 oz. lettuce, 6 chopped walnuts	9.0	10.6	19.8	263	5.2
3 prunes, canned, water-packed	6.4	.4	.1	30	2.8
Coffee with 1 T. cream	2.3	.9	3.0	40	5.7
	48.0	53.6	38.3	759	165.0
Total for Day	147.5	75.7	85.8	1723	320.0

MENU G

Breakfast	Carb.	Prot.	Fat	Cal.	Mg. Na.
4 oz. orange juice (½ cup)	11.3	.7	—	50	2.4
¼ cup oatmeal (1 oz.)	13.5	3.2	1.4	80	6.3
4 T. cream (20%)	2.3	1.7	12.0	124	22.8
1 sl. Low-Sodium Bread (Menu 1)	18.2	2.9	1.5	101	3.5
1 t. butter	—	—	2.8	27	.2
Coffee with 1 T. cream	2.3	.9	3.0	39	5.7
	47.6	9.4	20.7	421	40.9
Lunch					
Scrambled Egg and Mushrooms (Menu 1): Substitute 1 T. cream for milk	.6	7.1	11.0	133	76.8
Salad—½ grapefruit, 1 oz. lettuce	5.5	.9	.1	28	4.7
Cherry and Banana Gelatin (Menu 25). *Note:* Use Standard can of cherries in recipe. Do not use the Choice or Fancy brands	25.8	2.0	.2	115	47.6
Coffee with 1 T. cream	2.3	.9	3.0	39	5.7
	34.2	10.9	14.3	315	134.8
Dinner					
½ lb. broiled liver	5.8	46.9	12.4	310	195.2
4 oz. mashed yellow turnips	7.3	1.6	.2	40	5.6
Eggplant Mexican (Menu 25)	9.9	3.1	.7	57	23.2
Salad—2 oz. lettuce and 1 medium tomato	4.6	1.7	.7	31	10.0
Vinegar Dressing (4 t.): 1 T. vinegar and 1 t. sugar	5.0	—	—	20	3.0
Pineapple and Coconut (Menu 3): add	18.6	10.4	23.9	338	4.2
6 soft-shell chopped walnuts to this recipe	4.7	5.8	22.2	250	.6
Coffee with 1 T. cream	2.3	.9	3.0	39	5.7
	58.2	70.4	63.1	1085	247.5
Total for Day	140.0	90.7	98.1	1821	423.2

MENU H

Breakfast

	Carb.	Prot.	Fat	Cal.	Mg. Na.
4 oz. apricot nectar	11.3	.6	.2	50	2.0
¼ cup Instant Ralston (1 oz.) with	21.0	4.5	.5	110	.2
4 T. cream	2.3	1.7	12.0	124	22.8
1 sl. Low-Sodium Bread (Menu 1)	18.2	2.9	1.5	101	3.5
Coffee with 1 T. cream	2.3	.9	3.0	39	5.7
	55.1	10.6	17.2	424	34.2

Lunch

	Carb.	Prot.	Fat	Cal.	Mg. Na.
Spicy Creamed Egg (Menu 6)	8.0	10.1	14.0	215	106.5
1 mashed potato (3⅓ oz.)	18.0	2.2	.1	85	4.0
Salad—½ sliced apple, ½ sliced grapefruit on 1 leaf lettuce	11.6	1.1	.3	55	6.0
Coffee with 1 T. cream	2.3	.9	3.0	39	5.7
	39.9	14.3	17.4	394	122.2

Dinner

	Carb.	Prot.	Fat	Cal.	Mg. Na.
Beef Stew (Menu 4)	28.8	48.4	36.2	652	227.1
Baked potato (5 oz.)	38.1	4.6	.1	175	10.0
1 t. butter	—	—	2.8	27	.2
2 oz. hearts of lettuce	.5	.6	.2	6	6.8
4 t. Vinegar Dressing (Menu 25)	5.0	—	—	20	3.0
½ cup apple sauce, unsweetened: add	10.9	.3	.3	50	.4
6 soft-shell walnuts, chopped	4.7	5.8	22.2	250	.6
Coffee with 1 T. cream	2.3	.9	3.0	39	5.7
	90.3	54.8	64.8	1219	253.2
Total for Day	185.3	79.7	99.4	2037	409.6

MENU I

Breakfast	Carb.	Prot.	Fat	Cal.	Mg. Na.
4 oz. grapefruit juice (unsweetened)	10.2	.5	.1	45	.4
2 T. farina (⅔ oz.) (Do not use the quick-cooking type)	15.0	2.2	.1	70	.1
4 T. cream (20%)	2.3	1.7	12.0	124	22.8
1 sl. Low-Sodium Bread (Menu 1)	18.2	2.9	1.5	101	3.5
1 t. butter	—	—	2.8	27	.2
Coffee with 1 T. cream	2.3	.9	3.0	39	5.7
	48.0	8.2	19.5	406	32.7
Lunch					
1 scrambled egg in	—	6.7	5.2	75	67.0
1 t. butter	—	—	2.8	27	.2
2 oz. spaghetti	45.1	7.2	.2	219	4.4
Creole Sauce (Menu 7)	4.5	1.0	.4	26	5.0
Salad—2 oz. lettuce and ½ sliced orange with 3 chopped walnuts	6.4	5.8	10.1	143	8.0
Coffee* with 1 T. cream	2.3	.9	3.0	39	5.7
	58.3	21.6	21.7	529	90.3
Dinner					
Spanish Chicken (Menu 8)	25.7	57.4	18.6	506	193.3
French Fried Onions (Menu 8)	12.3	4.8	22.8	280	70.3
Boiled potato (3⅓ oz.)	18.0	2.2	.1	85	4.0
Salad—1 oz. cabbage, 1 oz. pineapple	4.2	.5	—	19	6.9
1 sl. Low-Sodium Bread (Menu 1)	18.2	2.9	1.5	101	3.5
Baked Apple (Menu 8)	12.2	.4	.5	55	2.6
1 T. cream (20%)	.6	.4	3.0	31	5.7
Coffee with 1 T. cream	2.3	.9	3.0	39	5.7
	93.5	69.5	49.5	1116	292.0
Total for Day	199.8	99.3	90.7	2051	415.0

SALT CONTENT OF 600 BASIC FOODS

The authorities referred to were those available to the author at the time of the first edition of this book. A quick glance across the table that follows demonstrates the fact that there is variation in the figures given by the various sources. The figures given by Henry C. Sherman and Peterson, Skinner and Strong are usually far in excess of those quoted by the other two authorities. They are given, despite misgivings as to their accuracy, because they have been so widely used and so long time-honored. McCance and Widdowson's figures are the result of careful chemical analysis, using the most recent chemical refinements. Mead Johnson's figures are obtained by the use of a flame photometer.

While there is occasional disparity between these last two authors, the magnitude of their differences is rarely as great as that between them and the other two authorities. We have used the higher figure in our computations as between McCance and Widdowson and Mead Johnson. Where neither McCance and Widdowson nor Mead Johnson provided the necessary figures, we have used those of Sherman or Peterson, Skinner and Strong.

In 1978 McCance and Widdowson published their fourth edition of *The Chemical Composition of Foods*. Compared to the earlier edition, some of the foods reflect some differences in sodium counts and many remain close to the same. The new recipes in this edition reflect some of these changes.

It may be noted that with boiling, many foods lose some of their sodium. However, this loss is sustained only if the liquor in which the food was boiled is not used. For example, an ounce of spinach contains 54.2 milligrams of sodium when fresh. After boiling, some sodium is dissolved in the liquor and the spinach contains only 34.9 milligrams per ounce. To retain this loss, the liquor must not be used.

If there is disagreement between McCance and Widdowson and Mead Johnson on processed or canned foods, Mead Johnson's figures have been taken, since the foods tested by them are of American manufacture whereas McCance et al. have tested foods in England.

Following are tables giving the sodium and caloric values of food per ounce, and consisting of a comparative listing of the sodium content as given by:

(A) R. A. McCance and E. M. Widdowson
   The Chemical Composition of Foods, 1947
   Chemical Publishing Co., Inc., Brooklyn, N.Y.
(B) Mead Johnson Research Laboratory, 1947
   Evansville, Ind.
(C) Henry C. Sherman Ph.D., Sc.D.
   Chemistry of Food and Nutrition, 1946
   The Macmillan Co., N.Y.
(D) Peterson, Skinner, Strong
   Elements of Food Biochemistry, 1943
   Prentice-Hall, Inc., N.Y.

In addition, the usual portions of food per person are given.
Parenthesis signifies amount is variable.
Tr—trace.
Sodium is given in milligrams per ounce.

List of Abbreviations

av.	average	mg.	milligram
btl.	bottle	Na.	sodium
bx.	box	oz.	ounce
cal.	calories	Prot.	proteins
Carb.	carbohydrates	pkge.	package
ch.	chop	pt.	pint
diam.	diameter	sl.	slice
gl.	glass	sm.	small
hd.	head	st.	stalks
lb.	pound	str.	strips
lrg.	large	T.	tablespoon
med.	medium	t.	teaspoon

NOTE: In the following tables all figures for sodium and calories are given per ounce.

Food	Usual Portions	Cal.	A	B	C	D
Ale, mild, bottled	1/2 pt. 8 oz.	17	6.8	2.2	—	—
Ale, pale, bottled	1/2 pt. 8 oz.	19	4.8	—	—	—
All-bran, Kellogg's	1 T. 1/9 oz.	88	(345)	400.0	—	6.8
Allspice, ground	—	—	—	17.7	—	—
Almonds	20 1 oz.	170	1.6	.5	7.4	6.8
Almonds, weighed with shells	—	63	.6	—	—	—
Almonds, roasted in oil and salt	—	—	—	45.7	—	—
Anchovy paste	1 t.	60	.6	3428.6	—	—
Apple	1 1/5 oz.	10	—	.02	2.8	4.2
Apple, dried	1 4 1/3 oz.	70	—	—	—	20.5
Apple juice	1/2 c. 2 oz.	12	—	1.14	—	—
Apple sauce, canned	1/2 c. 4 oz.	10	—	.09	—	—
Apricots	1 4 1/2 oz.	8	Tr.	.14	8.5	6.0
Apricots, canned	1/2 c. 5/6 oz.	17	.3	.5	—	—
Apricots, dried	5 4 oz.	52	16.0	—	7.1	31.1
Artichokes, Globe or French	1 1 2/3 oz.	4	—	—	—	—
Artichokes, Globe or French, boiled	1 1 2/3 oz.	5	4.2	—	—	—
Artichokes, Jerusalem	—	5	.7	—	—	—
Asparagus	1 3 1/3 oz.	—	—	—	—	—
Asparagus, boiled	6 2 1/2 oz.	6	.5	.5	4.5	2.2
Asparagus, canned	6 2 5/6 oz.	5	—	114.3	—	—
Asparagus, frozen	6 2 1/2 oz.	—	—	.8	—	—
Avocado	1/2 small 2 5/6 oz.	25	4.6	.5	—	—
Bacon	4 strips 2 2/3 oz.	115	(348)	217.1	19.1	—
Bacon, fried	4 strips 2/3 oz.	142	(800)	914.2	234.2	—
Bananas	1 med. 5 oz.	22	.3	.02	12.0	6.5
Bananas, weighed with skin	—	13	.7	—	—	—
Barley, pearl	3 T. 1 oz.	102	.2	.85	16.0	—
Barley, pearl, boiled	1/2 c. 3 1/3 oz.	34	21.3	—	—	—
Bass, steamed	—	36	11.3	—	—	—
Bass steamed, weighed with bone	1/2 lb.	19	(168)	—	—	—
Beans baked, canned	1 c. 8 oz.	26	5.6	—	—	—
Beans, broad, boiled	1/2 c. 4 1/6 oz.	12	17.4	—	—	—
Beans, butter	3/4 c. 2 1/2 oz.	76	—	—	—	—

BEANS TO
BRAZIL NUTS

Food	Usual Portions	Cal.	A	B	C	D
Beans, butter, boiled	1/2 c.	26	4.6			
Beans, green	1/2 c.	50		.23		3.4
Beans, green, canned	1/2 c.	6		117.1		
Beans, green, frozen	1/2 c.	6		.5		
Beans, Haricot	—	73	12.3			25.4
Beans, lima, green	1/2 c.	25	4.3	.28		
Beans, lima, canned	1/2 c.	38		88.0	47.7	
Beans, lima, dried	1/2 c.	97				80.5
Beans, Navy, dried	1/2 c.	106		.26		
Beans, string	3/4 c.	4	1.8		6.5	3.4
Beans, string, boiled	2/3 c.	2	.9			
Beef, corned, canned	1/4 lb.	66	(392)	485.7		
Beef, dried	1/8 lb.	55	1.4	1114.2		
Beef, drippings	1 T.	262	21.0			
Beef, frozen	1/3 oz.	43		15.1		
Beef, lean steak	1/2 lb.	50	19.6	15.0	24.0	18.8
Beer (see ale)	—					
Beets	2/3 c.	13		31.4	22.5	15.1
Beets, boiled	1/2 c.	13	18.2			
Beets, canned	1/2 c.	16		10.2		
Beets, leaves	1 c.	9		37.1		
Blackberries	2 oz.	8	1.1	.06	1.14	
Blackberries, stewed, no sugar	2/3 c.	4	.5			
Bloaters, grilled	—	73	(200)			
Bloaters, grilled, weighed with bone	1/4 lb.	(54)	(148)			
Blueberries	2/3 c.	15		.14	4.5	
Bluefish	1/2 lb.	26			19.4	
Bouillon cubes	1/7 oz.	5				
Bovril	1 t.	36	(1580)	7714.2		
Brain, calf, boiled	1/4 lb.	29	41.8			
Brain, pig	1/2 lb.	41		42.8		45.7
Brain, sheep, boiled	1/4 lb.	31	48.3			
Brandy	1 oz.	75	.4	.85		
Brazil nuts	4	183		.23	7.4	

Food	Measure		Wt.				
Brazil nuts, weighed with shells	—	—	82	.2	—	—	—
Brazil nuts, roasted in oil and salted	—	—	—	—	54.2	—	—
Bread, Passover (see Matzoh)							
Bread, rye and wheat	1 sl.	5/6 oz.	72	(112)	160.0	—	—
Bread, semi-whole wheat	1 sl.	1 oz.	72	(112)	191.4	—	—
Bread, white	1 sl.	5/6 oz.	75	(112)	191.4	127.4	147.7
Bread, whole wheat	1 sl.	1 oz.	70	(112)	122.8	6.8	8.5
Broccoli, tops	1 c.	4 oz.	10	—	4.5	—	—
Broccoli, tops, boiled	1/2 c.	3 1/3 oz.	4	1.9	—	—	—
Brussels sprouts	1 c.	3 1/3 oz.	16	—	3.1	—	—
Brussels sprouts, boiled	1/2 c.	3 1/3 oz.	5	2.2	—	—	—
Brussels sprouts, frozen	1/2 c.	3 1/3 oz.	5	—	2.5	—	—
Butter, average salted	1×1×1/2" or 1 T. melted	1/3 oz.	226	—	(280)	—	—
Butter, lightly salted	—	—	226	—	(222.8)	—	—
Butter, unsalted	1 c.	8 oz.	20	—	1.4	—	—
Buttermilk, cultured	1/2 c.	2 5/6 oz.	6	—	37.1	—	—
Cabbage, red	1 c.	4 oz.	7	9.0	1.4	9.1	10.8
Cabbage, Savoy	1/2 c.	3 1/3 oz.	3	6.4	1.4	9.1	10.8
Cabbage, Savoy, boiled	1/4	3 1/3 oz.	7	2.3	—	—	—
Cantaloupe melon	—	—	—	3.8	3.4	12.2	13.7
Cantaloupe melon, weighed with skin	1/2 c.	2 2/3 oz.	4	2.4	—	—	—
Caraway seed	1/2 c.	2 1/2 oz.	—	—	4.5	—	—
Carrots	2/3 c.	3 1/3 oz.	6	27.0	8.8	21.7	14.2
Carrots, boiled	8	1/2 oz.	5	14.2	—	—	—
Carrots, canned	1 T.	—	12	—	80.0	—	—
Cashew nuts	—	2/3 lb.	171	—	3.7	—	—
Cashew nuts, roasted and salted	—	1/2 lb.	200	—	57.1	—	—
Catsup, tomato	1 T.	1/4 lb.	37	—	371.4	—	—
Catfish	—	4 oz.	72	—	17.1	—	—
Catfish, steamed	—	3 1/3 oz.	34	30.6	—	—	—
Catfish, steamed, weighed with bone	—	3 1/3 oz.	28	26.0	—	—	—
Cauliflower buds	1 1/4 c.	4 oz.	8	—	6.8	—	—
Cauliflower buds, boiled	2/3 c.	3 1/3 oz.	3	3.2	6.2	11.7	13.7
Cauliflower buds, frozen	2/3 c.	3 1/3 oz.	3	—	—	—	—
Caviar, salmon	2 t.	1/2 oz.	100	—	628.5	—	—

CELERY TO CHICORY

Food	Usual Portions	Cal.	A	B	C	D
Celery salt	—	—	—	7428.5	—	—
Celery seed	—	—	—	40.0	—	28.8
Celery stalks	2 st.	3	38.9	31.4	37.1	—
Celery stalks, boiled	2/3 c.	1	18.9	—	—	—
Cereal—all-bran	1 T.	88	(345)	400.0	—	—
Cereal, wheat, Instant Ralston	1 oz.	110	—	.28	—	—
Cereal, wheat, Maltex	1 oz.	110	—	1.14	—	—
Cereal, wheat, Wheatena	1 oz.	110	—	.28	—	—
Chard, leaves and stalks	3 1/3 oz.	8	—	—	24.5	—
Cheese, American Swiss	oz.; sl. 1, 1 1/2 × 1 1/2 × 1 1/4", 1/8"	120; 105	120.0	—	—	—
Cheese, cheddar	5/6 oz.	120	—	154.2	—	—
Cheese, cottage	1 5/6 oz.	36	—	91.4	—	—
Cheese, cream	1 oz.	120	—	97.1	—	—
Cheese, Dutch	1 oz.	77	(355)	—	—	—
Cheese, Gorgonzola	1 × 1/2 × 2 1/2"	112	(347)	—	—	—
Cheese, Gruyere	2 × 1 × 1"	131	(154)	—	—	—
Cheese, process	1 oz.	118	(215)	428.5	—	—
Cheese, Parmesan	2 t.	—	—	—	—	—
Cheese, Stilton	5/6 oz., 1 1/2 × 1 1/2 × 1 1/4"	135	(326)	428.5	—	—
Cheese, whey (cheese food)	7 1/2 oz.	8	.8	.28	.85	4.2
Cherries, dark sweet	2 1/2 oz.	13	.7	—	—	—
Cherries, dark sweet, weighed with stones	—	11	—	—	—	—
Cherries, dark sweet, canned	2 5/6 oz.	44	—	.2	—	—
Cherries, dark, frozen in syrup	2 5/6 oz.	44	—	.28	—	—
Cherries, light sweet, canned	3 1/3 oz.	44	—	.85	—	—
Cherries, glacé	1/3 oz.	60	18.4	—	—	—
Chestnuts	3	49	3.1	.5	10.8	10.5
Chestnuts, weighed with shells	8	40	2.6	—	—	—
Chicken, boiled	1/4 lb.	58	27.8	—	—	—
Chicken, boiled, weighed with bone	—	38	18.1	—	—	—
Chicken, breast	1/2 lb.	46	—	22.2	—	—
Chicken, leg	1/2 lb.	47	22.7	31.4	26.0	15.4
Chicken, roast	1/4 lb.	54	12.2	—	26.0	15.4
Chicken, roast, weighed with bone	1/2 lb.	29	2.1	—	—	—
Chicory	1/4 sm. hd.	3	—	—	—	—

Food	Measure	Weight					
Chocolate, milk	3/4 × 1½ × 1/4"	1/5 oz.	167	(78)	24.5	—	—
Chocolate, plain	3/4 × 1½ × 1/4"	1/5 oz.	155	(41)	—	16.0	5.4
Chocolate, syrup	2 T.	1/2 oz.	80	—	.17	—	—
Chocolate, unsweetened	—	1/2 oz.	180	—	1.14	—	—
Cider, sweet	1 c.	8 oz.	17	—	1.14	—	—
Cinnamon, ground	—	—	—	—	2.2	—	—
Citron, candied	1/4	2½ oz.	100	—	82.8	172.4	—
Clams	6	2 oz.	25	—	51.4	—	—
Coca Cola	1 btl.	6 oz.	10	—	.28	—	—
Cocoa, ordinary	2 t.	1/6 oz.	128	(185)	—	—	—
Cocoa, Hershey's	—	—	—	—	1.14	—	17.1
Cocoa, powder, Dutch process	2 t.	1/6 oz.	178	8.1	15.7	16.8	—
Coconut, dry	1½ c.	3⅓ oz.	104	4.7	4.5	15.1	11.4
Coconut, fresh	1" square	1/3 oz.	10	29.8	—	11.1	—
Coconut, milk	1/2 c.	4 oz.	24	—	17.1	16.5	—
Cod	—	1/2 lb.	24	—	114.3	27.4	—
Cod, fillets, frozen	—	1/4 lb.	23	—	—	—	—
Cod, steamed	—	1/4 lb.	19	28.4	—	—	—
Cod, steamed, weighed with bones	—	—	—	23.0	—	—	—
Cod liver oil	1 T.	1/2 oz.	260	—	.02	—	—
Cod roe, fried	2 c.	2 oz.	59	36.0	—	—	—
Cod, salted	1/4 c.	1⅔ oz.	54	—	2057.1	—	—
Coffee	1 c.	8 oz.	1	Tr.	—	—	—
Corn, sweet white, canned	1/2 c.	3⅚ oz.	25	—	57.1	11.4	—
Corn, sweet white, milk stage	1 ear	3⅓ oz.	33	—	.06	11.4	—
Corn, sweet yellow, canned	1/2 c.	3⅚ oz.	25	—	60.0	11.4	—
Corn, sweet yellow, frozen	1 ear	3⅓ oz.	33	—	2.5	11.4	—
Corn, sweet yellow, milk stage	1 ear	3⅓ oz.	33	—	.09	11.4	—
Corn, yellow, dry	—	—	104	(298)	.11	—	—
Cornflakes	1⅓ c.	1 oz.	100	14.7	188.5	—	—
Cornflour	1 c.	4⅓ oz.	110	—	—	10.2	—
Cornmeal, yellow	1 T.	1/2 oz.	260	—	.17	11.1	—
Corn oil	1 T.	1/2 oz.	—	—	.06	—	—
Corn, popcorn, popped and oiled	1 c.	1/2 oz.	120	—	.85	—	—
Corn, popcorn, popped, oiled and salted	1 c.	—	120	—	428.5	—	—

Cornstarch to Eggplant

Food	Usual Portions		Cal.	A	B	C	D
Cornstarch	1/2 c.	2 oz.	110	—	1.14	—	—
Cowpeas	2/3 c.	3 1/3 oz.	41	—	.28	—	—
Cowpeas, dried	1/2 c.	3 1/3 oz.	105	—	—	—	10.2
Crab, boiled	—	2 oz.	36	104.0	—	—	—
Crab, boiled, weighed with shell	—	—	7	20.7	—	—	—
Crab, canned	1/2 c.	3 oz.	23	—	285.7	—	—
Cracker, graham	3	5/6 oz.	132	—	200.0	—	—
Cracker, soda	3	1/3 oz.	135	—	428.5	—	—
Cranberries	1/2 c.	1 2/3 oz.	4	.5	.28	1.7	.5
Cranberry sauce, canned	1/3 c.	3 1/3 oz.	55	—	.28	—	—
Cream	1 T.	1/2 oz.	115	9.0	11.4	(8.5)	8.8
Crisco	1 T.	1/2 oz.	220	—	1.14	—	—
Cucumber	2 1/2 × 2″	2 1/2 oz.	3	3.7	.23	2.8	7.4
Currants, black	1/2 c.	1 2/3 oz.	8	.8	.5	2.0	4.2
Currants, dried, black	1/3 c.	1 2/3 oz.	69	5.5	6.2	5.1	21.4
Currants, red	1/2 c.	1 2/3 oz.	6	.7	.5	2.0	4.2
Currants, white	1/2 c.	1 2/3 oz.	7	.4	—	2.0	4.2
Curry powder	1/5 t.	1/60 oz.	67	—	12.8	—	—
Dandelion	1/2 c.	1 2/3 oz.	18	—	21.7	48.0	—
Dates	3	1/2 oz.	70	1.4	.26	27.7	11.4
Dates, weighed with skin	—	—	61	1.2	—	—	—
Dill, seed	—	—	—	—	3.4	—	—
Duck, breast meat	—	1/2 lb.	48	—	19.4	—	—
Duck, leg meat	—	1/2 lb.	48	—	27.4	—	—
Duck, roasted	—	1/4 lb.	89	55.3	—	—	—
Duck, roasted, weighed with bone	—	—	48	29.8	—	—	—
Eels, elvers	—	1/2 lb.	20	19.0	—	—	9.1
Eels, silver	—	1/2 lb.	90	21.8	—	—	—
Eels, silver, weighed with bone and skin	—	1/2 lb.	60	14.5	—	—	—
Eels, yellow	—	1/2 lb.	49	25.3	—	—	—
Egg	1 av.	1 2/3 oz.	46	38.4	40.0	40.0	31.7
Egg, white	1 av.	1 1/6 oz.	11	54.7	57.1	48.5	50.0
Egg, yolk	1 av.	1/2 oz.	99	14.2	9.7	16.0	22.2
Eggs, dried	—	1 oz.	165	147.0	—	—	—
Eggplant	—	8 oz.	4	.7	.23	4.2	7.4

Food	Measure	Weight					
Endive	1/4 sm. hd.	1/2 oz.	3	2.9	5.1	17.1	—
Escarole	1/3 heart	1 2/3 oz.	3	—	—	17.1	—
Farina	2 T.	2/3 oz.	105	—	.23	18.5	—
Farina, quick-cooking, enriched	2 T.	2/3 oz.	103	—	28.5	—	43.1
Figs, canned in syrup	3	3 oz.	50	—	.28	—	12.2
Figs, dried	2 lrg.	1 1/2 oz.	61	24.6	9.4	18.8	—
Figs, green	1 lrg.	1 1/2 oz.	12	.5	.5	2.0	—
Filberts	20	1 1/6 oz.	214	—	.23	—	—
Flounder	—	1/2 lb.	18	—	—	—	—
Flounder, steamed	—	1/4 lb.	27	32.6	—	30.5	—
Flounder, steamed, weighed with skin and bones	—	—	—	—	—	—	—
Flour, bleached enriched, Gold Medal	3/4 c.	3 1/3 oz.	15	18.2	.28	—	—
Flour, bleached, phosphated enriched	3/4 c.	3 1/3 oz.	109	—	3.7	—	—
Flour, buckwheat	1 c.	4 oz.	109	—	.28	7.7	—
Flour, gluten	3/4 c.	3 1/3 oz.	102	—	.5	—	—
Flour, rye, dark	1 c.	3 1/3 oz.	103	—	.28	—	—
Flour, soya	1 c.	3 1/3 oz.	108	—	.17	—	—
Flour, white, natural	3/4 c.	3 1/3 oz.	84	.6	.28	12.8	15.1
Frog's legs	1 c.	1/2 lb.	100	.7	—	—	15.7
Fruit salad, canned in syrup	1 c.	4 1/3 oz.	19	—	2.5	—	—
Garlic	1 clove	—	20	—	1.7	—	2.5
Gelatin dessert, dry	1/4 bx.	5/6 oz.	120	—	94.2	—	—
Gelatin, plain	1 t.	1/10 oz.	100	—	7.7	—	—
Gin	1 c.	1 oz.	75	—	.2	—	—
Ginger ale	—	7 1/2 oz.	11	10.0	2.2	—	—
Ginger, ground	1 c.	—	74	—	—	—	—
Gluten, wheat	3/4 c.	3 1/3 oz.	103	—	8.2	—	—
Goose, roasted	—	1/4 lb.	92	41.2	.5	—	—
Goose, roasted, weighed with bone	—	—	53	23.8	—	—	—
Gooseberries	2/3 c.	3 1/3 oz.	5	—	.17	—	—
Grapes, black	20	3 1/3 oz.	17	.5	—	2.8	2.8
Grapes, white, seedless	30	3 1/3 oz.	18	.5	.28	3.1	3.1
Grape juice, sweetened, bottled	1/2 c.	4 oz.	—	—	1.14	3.1	3.1
Grapefruit	1/2 c.	3 1/3 oz.	6	.4	.11	1.14	1.7

GRAPEFRUIT TO KIDNEY, BEEF

Food	Usual Portions		Cal.	A	B	C	D
Grapefruit, whole fruit, weighed	—	—	3	.2	—	—	—
Grapefruit juice, sweetened, canned	1/2 c.	4 oz.	17	—	.11	1.4	—
Grapefruit juice, unsweetened, canned	1/2 c.	4 oz.	10	—	.11	1.4	—
Grapenuts	1/4 c.	1 oz.	102	(187)	—	—	—
Gravy flavoring	—	—	—	—	24.5	—	—
Haddock, fillets, raw	—	1/4 lb.	20	35.5	—	—	28.2
Haddock, steamed	—	—	28	34.4	—	—	—
Haddock, steamed, weighed with bones	—	—	21	26.2	—	—	—
Haddock, steamed and smoked	—	—	28	346.0	—	—	—
Halibut	—	1/2 lb.	40	—	16.0	31.7	—
Halibut, steamed	—	1/4 lb.	37	31.5	—	—	—
Halibut, steamed, weighed with bones	—	—	28	23.8	—	—	—
Ham, less excess fat	—	1/2 lb.	68	—	600.0	—	—
Ham, boiled, lean	—	1/4 lb.	62	(595)	—	—	—
Hare, roasted	—	1/4 lb.	55	15.0	—	—	—
Hare, roasted, weighed with bone	—	—	37	10.2	—	—	—
Hash, corned beef, canned	—	1/2 lb.	34	—	251.4	—	—
Hazelnuts	20	1 1/6 oz.	214	—	—	5.4	—
Heart, beef	—	1/4 lb.	74	—	25.7	43.7	29.1
Heart, sheep's, roasted	—	2 oz.	68	43.5	25.7	43.7	29.1
Heart, turkey	—	1 oz.	55	—	19.7	—	—
Herring	1 sm.	3 1/3 oz.	67	36.9	—	—	—
Herring, roe, fried	—	2 oz.	74	24.6	—	—	—
Hominy, canned	1/4 c.	1 2/3 oz.	108	—	51.4	—	—
Honey	1 T.	5/6 oz.	82	3.1	2.0	1.4	1.7
Honeycomb	—	—	80	2.0	—	—	—
Horseradish	2 t.	1/3 oz.	17	2.2	—	—	—
Horseradish, prepared	1 T.	1/10 oz.	100	—	27.4	—	26.8
Huckleberries	2/3 c.	3 1/3 oz.	15	—	—	4.5	—
Ice cream	—	2 1/2 oz.	58	18.2	—	—	—
Ice cream, vanilla	—	—	—	—	28.5	—	—
Jam, grape	1 t.	1/3 oz.	74	4.5	2.0	—	—
Jelly	1 t.	1/3 oz.	73	7.2	—	—	—
Kale	1 3/4 c.	6 oz.	14	—	31.4	14.8	14.2
Kidney, beef	—	5 oz.	34	69.5	60.0	65.7	68.0

Food	Measure	Weight					
Kidney, sheep	—	¼ lb.	34	71.0	—	—	—
Kippers, baked	—	2 oz.	57	281.0	—	—	—
Kippers, baked, with bone and skin	—	—	31	152.0	—	14.2	14.2
Kohlrabi	½ c.	1⅔ oz.	12	—	31.4	24.0	14.0
Lamb (see Mutton), less excess fat	1 ch.	3⅓ oz.	53	—	—	—	—
Lard	1 T.	½ oz.	262	.6	.09	—	10.2
Leeks	½ c.	1⅚ oz.	7	—	—	—	—
Leeks, boiled	¾ c.	3⅓ oz.	7	1.8	—	3.7	—
Lemons	1	3⅓ oz.	4	1.7	.17	—	—
Lemon juice	1 T.	½ oz.	2	.4	—	—	2.5
Lemon sole, steamed	—	¼ lb.	26	32.6	—	—	—
Lemon sole, steamed, weighed with skin and bone	—	—	—	—	—	—	—
Lentils	¼ c.	2 oz.	18	23.2	—	16.2	—
Lentils, boiled	½ c.	3⅓ oz.	84	10.2	—	8.5	—
Lettuce	2 lrg. lvs.	1⅔ oz.	27	2.7	3.4	—	8.0
Ling, steamed	—	¼ lb.	3	.9	—	—	—
Ling, steamed, weighed with bones	—	—	28	34.0	—	—	—
Litchi, dried	8 lrg. pits	⅚ oz.	21	25.5	.85	—	—
Liver, beef	—	½ lb.	90	24.4	—	24.8	6.0
Liver, beef, fried	—	¼ lb.	41	26.1	31.4	—	—
Liver, calf	—	½ lb.	81	—	—	24.8	—
Liver, calf, fried	—	¼ lb.	57	34.6	—	—	—
Liver, pig	—	½ lb.	74	—	22.0	—	—
Liver, turkey	—	3⅓ oz.	39	92.3	14.5	—	—
Lobster, boiled	1 av.	3⅓ oz.	42	33.2	60.0	—	—
Lobster, boiled, weighed with shell	—	—	34	—	—	—	—
Loganberries	⅔ c.	2½ oz.	12	.7	—	.5	—
Loganberries, canned	⅔ c.	4 oz.	5	.3	—	.5	—
Macaroni	½ c.	2½ oz.	29	—	.28	5.1	2.8
Macaroni, boiled	1 c.	8 oz.	32	2.2	—	—	—
Mace, ground	—	—	—	—	12.8	—	—
Mackerel	—	½ lb.	41	43.5	—	43.7	—
Mackerel, fried	—	¼ lb.	53	31.8	—	—	—
Mackerel, fried, weighed with bones	—	—	39	—	—	—	—
Malted milk	1 T.	¼ oz.	—	—	125.7	—	—

MALTED MILK
TO MULLET

Food	Usual Portions	Cal.	A	B	C	D
Malted milk, Horlick's	—	114	196.0	—	—	—
Maltex (see Cereals)						
Maple syrup	1 T., 3/5 oz.	85		4.0	3.1	
Margarine	1 T., 1/2 oz.	226	(90)	342.8		
Marmalade, orange	1 T., 5/6 oz.	74	5.2	3.7		
Matzoh, American-style	1–6" diam., 2/3 oz.	105		102.8		
Matzoh, egg				4.5		
Matzoh, farfel				8.0		
Matzoh, meal				1.14		
Matzoh, Passover				.28		
Matzoh, plain				.28		
Matzoh, poppy seed				100.0		
Matzoh, tasty wafer				122.8		
Matzoh, thin, tea				.5		
Matzoh, whole wheat				80.0		
Mayonnaise	1 T., 2/3 oz.	225		171.4		
Melon, cantaloupe	3 1/3 oz.	7	3.8	3.4	12.2	13.7
Melon, cantaloupe, weighed with skin	1/4	4	2.4			
Melon, yellow		6	5.5			
Melon, yellow, weighed with skin		4				
Milk, buttermilk, cultured	1 c., 8 oz.	20	3.5	37.1		
Milk, evaporated	1 T., 1/2 oz.	40		28.5		26.8
Milk, fresh, whole	1 c., 8 oz.	19	14.2	14.5	14.5	13.4
Milk, whole dry	2 T., 1/2 oz.	150	113.0	117.1		99.4
Milk, goat	1 c., 8 oz.	21		9.7		7.4
Milk, fresh, skimmed	1 c., 8 oz.	10	14.8			
Milk, condensed, whole, sweetened	1 T., 5/6 oz.	100	40.7			
Milk, condensed, whole, unsweetened	1 T., 5/6 oz.	44	45.8			
Milk, human, from 4 mothers 49 to 77 days postpartum		20		3.1		
Milk, human, from 9 mothers 3 to 10 days postpartum		20				
Molasses, cane	1 T., 5/6 oz.	80		11.4	12.2	
Mulberry	2/3 c., 2 1/2 oz.	10	.6	22.8		
Mullet, steamed	2 av., 1 2/3 oz.	36	26.6	.17		

Mullet, steamed, weighed with bone	—	—	23	17.0	—	—	—
Mushrooms	1/2 c.	1 2/3 oz.	2	2.6	1.4	7.7	3.7
Mushrooms, canned	1/2 c.	2 2/3 oz.	Tr.	—	134.2	—	—
Mussels	—	1/2 lb.	19	82.0	—	—	—
Mussels, boiled	—	—	25	59.8	—	—	—
Mussels, boiled, weighed with shells	—	—	7	17.9	—	—	—
Mustard, prepared	1 t.	1/3 oz.	30	—	314.2	—	—
Mustard, greens	1/2 c.	1 2/3 oz.	3	5.4	13.7	—	5.7
Mustard, powder	1 t.	1/6 oz.	132	1.0	.85	—	—
Mutton (see Lamb)							
Mutton chop, grilled, lean	1 ch.	3 1/3 oz.	77	36.0	—	—	—
Mutton chop, grilled lean, weighed with fat and bone	—	—	36	17.0	—	—	—
Mutton chop, grilled, lean and fat	1 ch.	3 1/3 oz.	142	29.0	—	—	—
Mutton chop, grilled, lean and fat, weighed with bone	—	—	108	21.8	—	—	—
Mutton leg, boiled	—	1/4 lb.	74	18.2	—	—	—
Mutton, leg, roast	—	1/4 lb.	83	20.1	—	—	—
Mutton chop, raw, lean	—	1/2 lb.	53	25.9	—	—	—
Mutton chop, raw, lean, weighed with bone	—	—	20	9.7	—	—	—
Nectarines	1	4 oz.	14	2.6	—	—	—
Nectarines, weighed with stones	—	—	13	2.4	—	—	—
Nutmeg, ground	—	—	—	—	4.0	—	—
Oatmeal	1/4 c.	1 oz.	115	9.5	.5	20.2	20.5
Okra	7–2 1/2" pods	1 2/3 oz.	7	—	.28	—	—
Oleomargarine	1 T.	1/2 oz.	226	(90)	342.8	—	—
Olives, green pickled	3	1/2 oz.	30	(639)	(628.5)	(339.7)	—
Olive oil	1 T.	1/2 oz.	264	Tr.	.06	—	—
Olives, ripe, pickled	3	1/2 oz.	50	—	262.8	—	—
Onions	1 med.	2 oz.	7	2.9	.28	4.2	5.7
Onions, boiled	5 sm.	2 1/2 oz.	4	1.9	—	—	—
Oranges	1 sm.	3 1/3 oz.	10	.8	.06	2.8	4.0
Oranges, weighed with peel and pips	—	—	8	.6	—	—	—
Orange Crush, soft drink	—	—	—	—	.5	—	—
Orange juice	1/2 c.	4 oz.	11	.5	.11	—	1.7

OVALTINE TO
PEPPER

Food	Usual Portions		Cal.	A	B	C	D
Ovaltine	1 T.	1/3 oz.	101	70.8	—	134.6	—
Oyster	6	4 oz.	14	143.0	20.8	—	—
Oyster, weighed with shells	—	—	2	17.2	—	—	—
Pancreas, pig	—	3 1/3 oz.	84	—	16.2	—	—
Paprika, powder	—	—	—	—	23.4	—	2.8
Parsley	1 t.	1/30 oz.	6	9.4	8.0	—	—
Parsnips, raw	3/4 c.	4 oz.	14	4.7	2.0	2.2	—
Parsnips, boiled	1/2 c.	2 2/3 oz.	16	1.2	—	—	—
Partridge, roast	—	1/4 lb.	60	28.4	—	—	—
Partridge, roast, weighed with bone	—	—	36	17.0	—	—	3.4
Peaches	2	5 oz.	11	.8	.02	4.2	—
Peaches, weighed with stones	—	—	9	.7	—	—	—
Peaches, canned	2 halves	4 2/3 oz.	19	.4	1.7	—	—
Peaches, dried	3	1 1/3 oz.	61	1.7	—	—	20.0
Peaches, frozen	2	5 oz.	—	—	.85	—	—
Peanuts	30	2 oz.	171	1.6	—	11.1	14.8
Peanut butter	1 T.	1/2 oz.	190	—	34.2	—	—
Peanut oil	1/2 c.	4 oz.	267	—	.06	—	—
Peanuts, roasted in oil and salted	—	—	—	—	131.4	—	—
Peanuts, roasted in shell	—	—	—	—	.23	—	—
Pears	1	4 oz.	12	.7	.5	2.2	2.8
Pears, weighed with skin and core	—	—	8	.5	—	—	—
Pears, canned	2 halves	4 oz.	18	.4	2.2	—	—
Peas	1/2 c.	2 1/2 oz.	18	.1	.26	5.4	6.8
Peas, boiled	1/2 c.	2 1/3 oz.	14	Tr.	—	—	—
Peas, canned	1/2 c.	2 1/3 oz.	24	(74)	65.7	25.4	—
Peas, dried	1/2 c.	3 1/3 oz.	78	10.8	—	—	—
Peas, dried, boiled	1/2 c.	4 oz.	28	3.6	—	—	—
Peas, frozen	1/2 c.	2 1/3 oz.	—	—	28.5	—	—
Peas, split, dried	1/2 c.	3 1/3 oz.	86	10.9	12.0	—	—
Peas, split, dried, boiled	1/2 c.	4 oz.	33	4.0	—	—	—
Pecans	6 whole	1 oz.	185	—	.06	—	—
Pepper, black ground (spice)	—	—	88	2.0	4.5	—	—
Pepper, green (vegetable)	3" piece	1 oz.	8	—	.14	—	4.2

Food							
Pepper, red (vegetable)	—	—	—	—	—	—	1.7
Pepper, red, ground (spice)	—	—	—	—	13.1	—	—
Pepper, white, ground (spice)	—	—	—	—	1.4	3.1	3.7
Persimmon	1 sm.	1⅔ oz.	24	—	.23	—	—
Pheasant, roast	—	¼ lb.	61	29.6	—	—	—
Pheasant, roast, weighed with bone	—	—	38	18.7	—	—	—
Pickle, dill	1 med.	1⅔ oz.	3	—	657.1	—	—
Pigeon, boiled	1 av.	6 oz.	62	21.0	—	—	—
Pigeon, boiled, weighed with bone	—	—	27	9.2	—	—	—
Pigeon, roast	1 lrg.	2⅔ oz.	66	29.8	—	—	—
Pigeon, roast, weighed with bone	—	—	29	13.1	—	—	—
Pike	—	½ lb.	24	—	—	—	—
Pineapple	1 c.	5 oz.	13	.5	.09	4.0	8.2
Pineapple, canned	2 sl.	5 oz.	18	.1	.28	—	2.2
Pineapple, frozen	—	—	—	—	.28	—	—
Pineapple juice, canned, unsweetened	½ c.	4 oz.	18	—	.11	—	—
Plums	2	2 oz.	11	.5	.02	1.14	.85
Plums, canned	3	3⅓ oz.	35	—	5.1	—	—
Pomegranate juice	½ c.	4 oz.	13	.3	.09	—	—
Popcorn, popped and oiled	1 c.	½ oz.	120	—	.85	—	—
Popcorn, popped, oiled and salted	—	—	120	—	428.5	—	—
Pork, less excess fat	—	—	90	—	16.5	19.7	23.1
Pork chops, grilled, lean	—	3⅓ oz.	92	18.8	—	—	—
Pork chops, grilled, lean, weighed with bone	1 ch.	½ lb.	38	21.6	—	—	—
Pork chops, grilled, lean and fat	1	3⅓ oz.	155	8.8	—	—	—
Pork chops, grilled, lean and fat, weighed with bone	—	—	128	16.8	—	—	—
Pork leg, roast	—	¼ lb.	90	13.9	—	—	—
Pork loin, roast, lean	—	¼ lb.	81	18.8	—	—	—
Pork loin, roast, lean and fat	—	¼ lb.	129	19.6	—	—	—
Pork loin, salt	—	2 oz.	240	17.0	828.5	—	—
Pork loin, salt and smoked	—	¼ lb.	69	511.0	—	—	—
Postum, cereal beverage	1 t.	1/15 oz.	105	—	10.2	—	—
Postum, instant, dry	1 t.	1/15 oz.	90	—	20.2	—	—
Potatoes, chips	1⅓ c.	1 oz.	175	—	97.1	—	—

POTATOES TO RUTABAGAS

Food	Usual Portions		Cal.	A	B	C	D
Potatoes, sweet, boiled	1 med.	3⅓ oz.	23	5.1	—	—	—
Potatoes, sweet, canned	2 sm.	1½ oz.	90	—	13.7	—	8.8
Potatoes, sweet, less skin	1-6"	5 oz.	36	2.0	1.14	7.7	8.5
Potatoes, white	1 med.	4 oz.	24	1.0	.17	6.8	—
Potatoes, white, boiled	—	—	23	—	—	—	—
Potatoes, white, canned	—	—	—	—	100.0	—	—
Potatoes, white, fried	—	—	68	3.3	—	—	—
Poultry seasoning	—	—	—	—	7.4	—	—
Pretzels	6 med.	1 oz.	95	—	314.2	—	—
Prunes, canned	3	3⅓ oz.	30	3.5	.85	22.2	28.8
Prunes, dried	8 lrg.	3⅓ oz.	46	2.9	1.4	—	—
Prunes, dried, weighed with stones	—	—	38	—	—	—	—
Prune juice, unsweetened	½ c.	4 oz.	17	.4	.5	15.4	3.1
Pumpkin	¾ c.	4 oz.	4	—	.11	—	—
Pumpkin, canned	½ c.	4 oz.	10	—	.5	—	—
Quail, breast meat	—	—	—	—	10.0	—	—
Quail, leg meat	—	—	—	—	12.5	—	—
Quinces	1	8 oz.	7	.9	.17	—	—
Rabbit, foreleg	—	½ lb.	35	—	13.4	—	13.4
Rabbit, loin	—	½ lb.	37	—	9.7	—	13.4
Rabbit, stewed	—	¼ lb.	51	9.1	—	—	—
Rabbit, stewed, weighed with bone	—	—	26	4.6	—	—	—
Radishes	6 med.	1⅔ oz.	4	16.8	2.3	18.2	23.7
Raisins	½ c.	2½ oz.	70	14.9	6.2	24.8	34.2
Raspberry, black	⅔ c.	2½ oz.	18	—	.06	—	—
Raspberry, red	⅔ c.	2½ oz.	7	.7	.11	.85	2.0
Raspberry juice	½ c.	4 oz.	14	—	—	1.4	—
Rhubarb, raw	1 c.	3 oz.	2	.6	.28	4.8	2.8
Rhubarb, stewed without sugar	⅔ c.	3⅓ oz.	1	.4	—	—	—
Rice flakes	1 c.	1 oz.	120	—	205.7	—	—
Rice, puffed	1 c.	½ oz.	120	—	.23	—	—
Rice, polished and coated	1 T.	⅔ oz.	102	1.8	.5	8.0	3.4
Rice, boiled	½ c.	3⅓ oz.	35	.6	1.14	—	—
Rice, vitaminized	—	—	102	—	.5	—	—
Rum	—	1 oz.	75	—	—	—	—
Rutabagas	¾ c.	3 oz.	14	—	1.4	—	14.8

Rye flour (see Flour)

Food							
Sage	1/4 c.	1 1/3 oz.	—	—	5.4	24.0	26.5
Sago	—	8 oz.	101	1.0	—	—	—
Salmon	1/2 c.	3 1/3 oz.	60	—	13.7	—	—
Salmon, canned	—	4 oz.	60	(152)	134.2	—	—
Salmon, steamed	—	—	57	30.4	—	—	—
Salmon, steamed, weighed with bones	—	—	46	24.7	—	—	—
Salt	—	—	—	11,000.0	11,240.5	—	—
Sardines, herring, canned in oil	4–2 1/2" long	1 2/3 oz.	84	(223)	145.7	—	—
Sardines, pilchard, canned in natural sauce	—	2 oz.	54	(169)	217.1	—	—
Sardines, pilchard, canned in tomato sauce	—	3 oz.	40	—	114.3	—	—
Sauerkraut, canned	2/3 c.	3 1/3 oz.	6	—	208.5	—	—
Sausage, bologna	6 sl.	2 1/2 oz.	72	—	62.8	—	—
Sausage, Frankfurt	2–7 × 3/4"	4 oz.	78	—	314.2	—	—
Sausage, pork	2–3 1/2" long	1 1/6 oz.	97	(218)	314.2	—	—
Sausage, pork, fried	—	2 oz.	93	(284)	—	—	—
Scallops, steamed	1/2 c.	3 1/3 oz.	30	75.3	—	—	—
Shortening, vegetable, Crisco	1 T.	1/2 oz.	220	—	1.14	—	—
Shortening, vegetable	1 T.	1/2 oz.	220	—	.11	—	—
Shredded Wheat	1 biscuit	1 oz.	103	4.7	.5	—	—
Shrimps	8 med.	2 oz.	32	—	40.0	—	—
Skate, fried	—	4 oz.	69	51.8	—	—	—
Skate, fried, weighed with bones	—	—	57	42.9	—	—	—
Smelts, fried	3	3 1/3 oz.	116	42.0	—	—	—
Smelts, fried, weighed with bones	—	—	98	35.7	—	—	—
Soda, baking, theoretical value for pure NaHCO3	—	—	—	—	(7,820.8)	—	—
Sole, lemon, steamed	—	4 oz.	26	—	114.3	—	—
Sole, lemon, steamed, weighed with bones	—	—	18	—	114.3	—	—
Soup, beef, canned, diluted as served	1/2 c.	4 oz.	21	32.6	—	—	—
Soup, tomato, canned, diluted as served	1/2 c.	4 2/3 oz.	18	23.2	—	—	—
Soup, vegetable, canned, diluted as served	1/2 c.	4 2/3 oz.	24	—	42.8	—	—
Soybean, dry	1/2 c.	3 1/3 oz.	120	—	1.14	—	—
Spaghetti (see Macaroni)	—	—	—	—	—	—	—
Spinach	1 1/4 c.	2 1/2 oz.	6	—	54.2	—	—

Spinach to Tongues

Food	Usual Portions	Cal.	A	B	C	D
Spinach, boiled	½ c.	7	34.9	—	—	—
Spinach, canned	1 c.	7	—	85.7	—	—
Spinach, frozen	1 c.	7	—	17.1	—	—
Sprats, fried	—	126	37.5	—	—	—
Sprats, fried, weighed with heads	2 oz.	111	33.0	—	—	—
Sprats, smoked, grilled	2 oz.	91	(240)	—	—	—
Sprats, smoked, grilled, weighed with heads	—	81	(213)	—	—	—
Squab, see Pigeon						
Squash, acorn	4 oz.	13	—	.09	—	3.1
Squash, hubbard	4 oz.	13	—	.06	—	3.1
Squash, yellow, summer	4 oz.	6	—	.14	—	3.1
Squash, white	1¾ c.	6	—	.06	.5	3.1
Strawberries	¾ c.	7	.4	.2	2.0	—
Strawberries, frozen, sweetened	3⅓ oz.	40	—	.5	—	—
Sturgeon, steamed	¾ c.	44	30.6	—	—	—
Sturgeon, steamed, weighed with bones	4 oz.	30	20.8	—	—	—
Suet	1 T.	262	6.0	6.8	—	—
Sugar, light brown	1 T.	105	—	—	—	—
Sugar, white	1 T.	112	.1	.09	—	—
Sweetbreads, stewed	2 oz.	51	19.6	—	—	—
Sweet potatoes (see Potatoes)						
Syrup, chocolate	2 T.	80	—	17.1	3.1	—
Syrup, maple	1 T.	85	—	4.0	—	—
Syrup, sorghum	1 T.	75	—	5.7	—	—
Syrup, table, corn and cane	5⅓ oz.	92	—	23.7	—	—
Tangerines	½ c.	10	.6	.5	—	—
Tangerines, weighed, with skin	2–2″ diam.	7	.4	—	—	—
Tangerines, juice, sweetened, canned	¼ c.	12	1.2	.17	1.14	—
Tapioca	1⅓ c.	102	1.14	1.4	—	—
Tea (infusion)	—	Tr.	—	—	—	—
Thyme, whole	—	—	—	10.2	—	—
Tobacco, chewing	1 sm.	—	.8	457.1	—	—
Tomatoes	4 oz.	4	—	5.1	5.7	3.7
Tomatoes, canned	4⅓ oz.	6	—	65.7	—	—
Tomato juice, canned	4 oz.	6	—	28.5	4.2	—

Tongues, beef, pickled	—	2	oz.	88	532.0	—	—	—
Tongues, lamb, stewed	—	4	oz.	84	22.5	—	—	—
Tripe, pickled	—	4	oz.	18	—	13.1	—	—
Tripe, stewed	—	4	oz.	29	20.4	—	—	—
Trout, steamed	—	4	oz.	38	25.0	—	—	—
Trout, steamed, weighed with bones	—			25	16.5	—	—	—
Trout, sea, steamed	—	4	oz.	37	58.7	—	—	—
Trout, sea, steamed, weighed with bones	—			29	46.3	—	—	—
Tuna, canned	1/2 c.			87	—	154.2	—	—
Turkey, breast meat	—	3	oz.	86	—	11.4	37.1	37.1
Turkey, leg meat	—	8	oz.	86	—	26.2	37.1	37.1
Turkey, roast	—	8	oz.	56	36.9	—	—	—
Turkey, roast, weighed with bone	—	4	oz.	34	22.1	—	—	—
Turnips, white	3/4 c.	4	oz.	5	16.5	10.5	18.8	29.7
Turnips, boiled	1/2 c.	4	oz.	3	8.0	—	—	—
Turnips, leaves	1 c.	3⅓	oz.	11	—	2.8	12.8	74.2
Turnips, yellow (see Rutabagas)	1/2 c.	3⅓	oz.	3	1.9	—	—	—
Vanilla extract	1 t.			12	—	.28	—	—
Veal	—	8	oz.	31	30.4	13.7	25.4	24.5
Veal, frozen	—	8	oz.	31	27.0	—	—	—
Veal, cutlet, fried	1 av.	2⅔	oz.	61	30.1	—	—	—
Veal, fillet, roast	—	4	oz.	66	27.5	—	—	—
Venison, roast	—	4	oz.	56	24.4	—	—	20.0
Vinegar, cider	1 t.	1/6	oz.	1	6.0	.28	5.7	—
Vinegar, distilled	—			—	—	.17	—	—
Walnuts, black	6	1⅙	oz.	201	—	.5	6.5	3.7
Walnuts, English	6	1⅙	oz.	156	.8	.5	—	—
Walnuts, English, weighed with shells	—			100	.5	—	—	—
Watercress	1/2 c.	2/3	oz.	4	17.0	—	22.8	8.8
Watermelon	1 c.	8	oz.	9	—	.09	5.7	3.4
Wheatena (see Cereal)	1 c.			—	—	—	—	—
Wheat flakes	1 c.	1	oz.	110	—	285.7	—	—
Wheat germ, containing some bran and flour	1/4 c.	1	oz.	109	—	.5	—	—

Food	Usual Portions		Cal.	A	B	C	D
Wheat, puffed	1 c.	½ oz.	110	—	.85	—	—
Wheat, shredded	1 biscuit	1 oz.	103	4.7	.5	—	—
Whisky, blended	1 brandy gl.	1 oz.	85	—	.09	—	—
Whisky, bonded		1 oz.	85	—	.02	—	—
Whiting, steamed		4 oz.	26	36.1	—	—	—
Whiting, steamed, weighed with bones		—	17	24.5	—	—	—
Wine, port	1 wine gl.	3⅓ oz.	49	—	1.14	2.2	—
Wine, sauternes		3⅓ oz.	24	—	2.8	—	—
Wineberry			—	—	.23	—	—
Worcestershire sauce	1 t.	⅙ oz.	24	—	400.0	—	—
Yeast, compressed	1½" square	⅗ oz.	25	—	1.14	—	—
Yeast, debittered, dry			—	—	51.4	—	—
Yeast, primary, cultured dry			—	—	8 to 320	—	—
Zwieback	1-3×1¼"	⅙ oz.	120	—	71.4	—	—

Index to Recipes